"In a world where we all wish to belong, we rarely have the gift of truth-tellers naming how hard it can be to truly find community, love, and compassion. Rev. Hinton Hill gives us a window into her soul in *Love, Auntie*. Her transparency reminds us that we are not alone, and the parables and prayers assure us that belonging is a journey, not a destination. She guides us through the highs and lows of our search for belonging and assures us that we matter. Run, don't walk, to your local bookseller to pick up this book."

—**REV. DR. GABBY CUDJOE WILKES**, pastor and author of *Psalms for Black Lives: Reflections for the Work of Liberation*

"The concept of sacred belonging is a gentle and warm call toward love. Even if you've never met Shantell Hinton Hill, you can feel her evolution throughout this book. *Love, Auntie* is a tender hug after what feels like an excruciating decade for this country and its people. I cannot wait for the world to receive this book with open hearts."

—**PRISCA DORCAS MOJICA RODRÍGUEZ**, author of *For Brown Girls with Sharp Edges and Tender Hearts: A Love Letter to Women of Color* and *Tías and Primas: On Knowing and Loving the Women Who Raise Us*

"Shantell Hinton Hill's *Love, Auntie* is a necessary and bold love letter to all of us. It drips in gorgeous womanist insistence on the world we could have. Her moving linguistic artistry—which calls on us to tell the truth, discern what is, heal what can be healed, and survive and create sanctuary in the best and most radical ways possible—is beautiful and precise."

—**TAMURA LOMAX**, PhD, associate professor of religious studies at Michigan State University and author of *Jezebel Unhinged: Loosing the Black Female Body in Religion and Culture*

"Rev. Shantell Hinton Hill's *Love, Auntie* is a practical, prayerful, and powerful invitation into the fullness of our God-given humanity through community, justice, and faithful curiosity. Hinton Hill reminds us that vulnerable leadership is powerful, and she shares her own experiences—pains she carries, mistakes she's made, transformations she has undergone, skills she has developed—in a practice of caretaking and wisdom-sharing. What an absolute gift: this book is part memoir, part devotional practice, and one hundred percent a Womanist companion for building justice and faithfulness simultaneously."

—**LYNDSEY GODWIN**, program operations coordinator at SACReD Dignity and adjunct professor at Vanderbilt Divinity School

Love,
Auntie

Parables and Prayers for Sacred Belonging

Shantell Hinton Hill

HERALD
PRESS

Harrisonburg, Virginia

Herald Press
PO Box 866, Harrisonburg, Virginia 22803
www.HeraldPress.com

Library of Congress Cataloging-in-Publication Data
Names: Hinton Hill, Shantell, author.
Title: Love, auntie : parables and prayers for sacred belonging / Shantell
    Hinton Hill.
Description: Harrisonburg, Virginia : Herald Press, [2024] | Includes
    bibliographical references.
Identifiers: LCCN 2024025107 (print) | LCCN 2024025108 (ebook)
    | ISBN 9781513814544 (paperback) | ISBN 9781513814551 (hardcover)
    | ISBN 9781513814568 (ebook)
Subjects: LCSH: Love—Religious aspects—Christianity. | Social
    acceptance—Religious aspects—Christianity. | Interpersonal
    relations—Religious aspects—Christianity. | Christian life. | BISAC:
    RELIGION / Christian Living / Social Issues | SELF-HELP / Spiritual
Classification: LCC BV4639 .H454 2024 (print) | LCC BV4639 (ebook)
    | DDC 248.4—dc23/eng/20240711
LC record available at https://lccn.loc.gov/2024025107
LC ebook record available at https://lccn.loc.gov/2024025108

Study guides are available for many Herald Press titles at
www.HeraldPress.com.

LOVE, AUNTIE
© 2024 by Herald Press, Harrisonburg, Virginia 22803. 800-245-7894.
    All rights reserved.
Library of Congress Control Number: 2024025107
International Standard Book Number: 978-1-5138-1454-4 (paperback);
    978-1-5138-1455-1 (hardcover); 978-1-5138-1456-8 (ebook)
Printed in United States of America
Design by Merrill Miller
Elements of cover illustration from Getty Images

Unless otherwise noted, Scripture text is quoted, with permission, from
the *New Revised Standard Version Updated Edition*, Copyright © 2021
National Council of Churches of Christ in the United States of America.
Used by permission. All rights reserved worldwide. Scripture quotations
marked (KJV) are taken from the King James Version. Scripture marked
(NMB) is taken from the New Matthew Bible, copyright © 2016 by Ruth
Magnusson (Davis). All rights reserved.

28 27 26 25 24   10 9 8 7 6 5 4 3 2 1

Contents

Foreword

BLACK FOLK CULTURE IS OFTEN celebrated for its colloquial expressions and extended village. Our storytelling is awash in wit and wisdom, belly laughs and biting clapbacks, and tales that will "make you wanna holla" and "throw your hands up in the air," as a way of bringing a little bit of heaven down to earth when everything is out of hand. Likewise, our extended village is so vast that it crosses borders, breaks ceilings, and tears down walls in an effort to widen the circle of divine territory and social influence. These expressions and extensions of our culture prepare family feasts of soul food while always making room for people to be spirit helpers who not only include others but promote them.

And no one does this better than "Auntie."

One of the most popular and motherland-retained expressions within our extended village is "Auntie." While this term was always used with kinfolk and skinfolk (those related not necessarily by blood but by love), it has spread and taken hold everywhere, from popular culture to the pews at church, and even the political arena. When US representative Maxine Waters attained "Auntie" status in the spring of 2017, young Black people who were more used to hearing negative references to Black women renamed the congresswoman "Auntie

Maxine"—"in response to her witty, acerbic, and wise comments about Donald Trump." As scholar Imani Perry wrote, "A digital public sphere, horrified by [the president's] behavior, delighted in Waters' [rebuke]."[1] And while I, like many of my Black female professional colleagues, have been stressed by and utterly shunned such familial references from our students, colleagues, or clientele because we neither wanted to be a caricature nor a codger, something new emerged when we would hear young people say, "That one right there, she's a real one. She's an auntie for real!"

As a self-avowed "Auntie," Shantell Hinton Hill draws on the best of our cultural expressions of storytelling and extends her love to an audience that is unbeknownst to her. In this accessible volume, we get from this brilliant mind, large heart, and storytelling genius womanist wisdom rightly divided as a word of truth that meets her audience where they long to be, drawn out from the world that is vast and renders them invisible and brings them onto a porch for a cool drink of everlasting sweet tea and shade that gives relief—but will also put you in check.

You see, in the Black tradition, "Auntie" functions as the "Un-tie." The elder who partners in spiritual parenting with womanish wisdom and loves the children into wholeness from the stereotypical and salacious lies of a racist, sexist, classist, and misogynoir society, which would dare to suggest that their Blackness and "womanish" or "mannish" ways are anything less than divine evidence that they were and are fearfully and wonderfully made.

And though they are not necessarily womb bearers or legal guardians of the younger generation, Aunties see themselves as spiritual custodians and the youth of our age as their walking heart, because a walking heart does not just remain hidden away in blood and bone! Here, I cannot help but echo "What manner of woman is this?"—as in the mystery and necessity of such women, such as the woman in the gospel story who takes her most prized possession of perfume and trespasses into sacred space to anoint Jesus and prepare him for the most horrible and honorable moment in his life. Or "What manner of love is this?"—as in 1 John 3:1, which asks what manner of love would be so divine as to claim others as their own divine children.

That quality of selfless love is incomprehensible to most humans. But not Aunties. The "young'uns" or "young guns" are their walking hearts because they exist outside of them yet walk with and around them daily—taking their entire race, irrespective of region, class, or tone, to places outside oneself and going above and beyond what could ever be imagined. That heart is a lifeline to what Hinton Hill calls "sacred belonging," and the parables and prayers she offers on her stacked porch house not only spark interest for seeing womanism and intergenerational dialogue in a novel way, but also tender an intimate invitation to bring people in from the outside via the four womanist tenets that I named as "radical subjectivity, traditional communalism, redemptive self-love, and critical engagement."

Having first met Hinton Hill years ago as my mentee (and definitely not as her Auntie), I am deeply moved by how she has refashioned herself as "Auntie" in this volume. She makes womanist theory more palpable and personal as she culls from theory an actual lived space of four "porch talks" where passersby can feel at home. *Now, mind you, every reader will get called out, but it's only to draw you closer into community.*

In *Love, Auntie*, Hinton Hill does much more than just talk the talk of our culture—like a good Auntie, she walks the walk with her readers through a series of epistles (sacred talk for letters) that invite all her children of interest, even those with "hard heads," to take on "a defiant posture and audacious, inquisitive nature"; heed "the practical wisdom and common sense of Black women"; "esteem and reclaim the unique aesthetic aspects of Black femininity that normative society usually disparages," and "transform society by imparting a liberating vision of a just and inclusive world."

Welcome, beloved community of all shades of skinfolk, to "this here" stacked porch where your mind, body, and soul will be wrapped in attention that may not only save souls, but save lives and minds in the process! Brace yourself, but embrace and enjoy this text because you will relish in its womanish expression and extension of all that is fearfully and wonderfully yet in the making.

—Stacey M. Floyd-Thomas
E. Rhodes and Leona B. Carpenter
Chair and Professor of Ethics and
Society at Vanderbilt University

Preface

To my Belongings,

I have seen you in your childhood. I saw the harm that still lingers in your body. I know who you are becoming. And who you've fought to leave behind. I speak healing over your future. Anti-Blackness, misogynoir, and self-hatred of any kind will not serve you where you are going. I will tell you the many truths about the terrors we face. But I will help you find the way to your highest and most faithful self so that those terrors do not consume you. I call forth joy and rest and wonder into your being. To replace trauma and burnout and hopelessness. And I am committed to walking with you until you see the divine goodness you are meant to be. So, beloved . . . find comfort here. Find humor and hope and honor here. Find and gather your-selves here. Find a community of belonging here. This space is for you to come home to being whole, safe, and seen. You and your fullness are welcome here anytime.

—love, Auntie.

IN EARLY 2022—on an otherwise ordinary day in the middle of the pandemic—I wrote these words. I wrote them from a place of loneliness and longing. Of creativity and curiosity borne from both incalculable loss and unspeakable joy. I wrote these words in the incredibly happy and hard season of postpartum depression after the miraculous birth of my daughter and untenable grief after the unexpected death of my bonus dad. I wrote these words because I needed somewhere for my faith to go. I needed some way to write myself back into feeling and find a holding space for all the pieces left of who I'd once been. I wrote these words as an SOS and posted them on a social media account, just hoping someone else would see them and save me. Help me make sense of a world that just didn't make sense anymore and feed a starving faith that could no longer provide nourishment to my grief-stricken body. I was both desperate and determined to search for this place my soul longed for; and what started as a cry for help somehow became a means of discovering the beginnings of sacred belonging.

Sacred belonging is both a call to action and a call to community. First, it is an invitation to reconcile your (un)becoming—that is, the shedding of who you once were—and the evolution of faith identity that follows soul-leveling disruptions. Next, it is an invocation to request God's power and presence as you journey toward being in right relationship with others and yourself. Sacred belonging is a process that allows you to make peace with the tools you had that once helped you survive where you were while accepting that there is more for you to learn as you grow into who God is asking you to be. Most of all, sacred belonging is a wholehearted belief that says: I deserve to have a faith that makes room. A faith that makes room for me—*all* of me. For you—*all* of you. For those on the margins. For the oppressed. For the expansiveness of who God is and who God will be. For a just-filled world that is already at hand yet is still to come.

Finally, a sacred belonging is what I call you, dear one. I may not know your name, but I know part of your story. I know you are here, reading this book, because you want to find a better way to do life with a faith that handles all of who you are. I know you have been harmed, or have caused harm, because of religious teachings passed down to you. I know you are on a journey that scares you and excites you at the same time. I hope you will know that you are so worth this time and labor.

In a time when we are all caught in the crosshairs of culture wars, the constant consumption found in a capitalistic world, dangerous religious and political rhetoric, and economic chaos rife with racial and social upheaval, I hope you will transform this moment in history into the most revelatory and revolutionary season of your life. This book, I pray, will help you on your journey to wrest yourself away from old ways of thinking and stagnated patterns of theology that have made closed-mindedness your weapon of choice. This book is a guide to getting free of the chains that have kept you bound to problematic belief systems rooted in oppression and dressed up as a polite profession of faith that causes more harm than good. In these pages, you will find different modes of biblical interpretation, faith practice, and spiritual accountability to usher you into a new era of personal and public witness as a person of faith. This is the answer to the silent SOS you've been praying, either in the form of tears or words, that will affirm that there is room to be a person of deep faith who is also devoted to social justice and anti-oppression principles. May this book be a new testament in the unfolding gospel of your life—one that reminds you that all of who you are is a sacred belonging.

From My Front Porch

An Invitation to Sacred Belonging and a Word about Aunties

I'VE NEVER REALLY BEEN A HUGE FAN OF CHANGE. I enjoy things being predictable. At stasis. Safe, to a certain degree. However, my relationship with change shifted once I accepted disruption as an opportunity to find sacred belonging. And if we're keeping it real, it was not that I accepted it. Rather, it was forced upon me. The TL;DR version of the story is that when I was just shy of thirty years old, I was forced to leave certain elements of biblical fundamentalism behind when my then-pastor refused to acknowledge my call to ministry. The longer version: I'd been actively serving in my church, building our nearly defunct youth ministry faithfully, but when I began to discern the voice of God saying there was more for me—this pastor sat me down and walked me through every single text in the New Testament having to do with women remaining *silent* in the church. A denominational and doctrinal brand of literal interpretation of the Bible encouraged this behavior from my then-pastor. And no matter how damaging or damning his indictment against the very nature of an omnipotent God, he felt justified in silencing God's voice and work in my life.

That incident began a long journey of unlearning and unwinding myself from beliefs that I'd been taught my entire life. Beliefs about gender roles and "what the Bible says" that had become the major tendons supporting the muscles of my faith were now snapped like the ACL I tore playing basketball in my junior year of high school. The same way I couldn't keep playing on a bad knee until the tendon was repaired, I could not carry on with a faith that could no longer carry me.

You know how utterly confusing and chaotic it felt when the COVID-19 pandemic first began? Like life as we knew it was over and we had to face isolation, fear, and the unknown, all in one fell swoop? That's how it felt when I began the process of asking the "what now" questions regarding my faith. Many of us have begun trudging down that lonely road of navigating a whole new (scary) world as it relates to our faith beliefs and practices. Maybe it started for you because of something catastrophic (like the experience with my former pastor) or because some curiosity inside of you invited it. Either way, the process of (un)becoming has, perhaps, led you to grapple with sacred belonging—even if you have not had the language to call it that.

In the ten years that have flown by since that incident with my former pastor, I have come to find that most people who go on this journey of *faith to faith* (as in Romans 1:17 [KJV]; also, as in former faith to more informed faith) can be categorized into four broad categories:

Deconstructors—Those who are actively attempting to wrest themselves away from damaging or toxic theologies. They are usually highly critical of the church and evangelicalism and have found community among affinity groups—which allows them to share their critiques of Westernized religion with people who share their sentiments.

Doubters—Those who have plummeted from being persons of faith to questioning the existence of a higher power.

Doubters are often torn between head and heart and have a hard time reconciling their intellect with their spirituality. Additionally, a growing number of doubters do not suffer from disbelief; rather, they view their existential and theological questions as an integral part of their faith.

Re-memberers—Those who have experienced harm in the very religious institutions that reared them yet are determined to use the fragments of goodness that remain to challenge their faith (and faith-based institutions) to become better.

Relishers—Those who understand spirituality as a key ingredient to the human experience and cherish the opportunity to explore and expand their faith in relationship with others or themselves. Relishers are often quite open to learning; they value embodied reflection and thoughtful provocation wherever they may find it.

As I've journeyed through my own process of deconstructing and regathering my spirituality, I have been in virtually every category of faithful exploration—from deconstructor to relisher. And I remain deeply fond of each of those periods in my life.

My deconstructor phase began with that disruptive event with my former pastor. From that moment, I went looking for a soft and healing place to land—a sacred belonging that would not cause more injury to my fractured faith and would help repair me my faith as gently as possible. In that time, I found myself attending small nondenomintional churches, trying to accept myself, until I was eventually accepted into seminary. And that divine orchestration not only reordered my life but also my thinking about what needed repair. Where I thought my faith would be restored—as in surgically repaired like my torn ACL—it was not. Instead, I learned it was not my faith that had to be fixed. Rather, my heart had to be fixed—it needed to be completely convinced that my faith could go beyond the frailties of human limitations and oppressive ideologies.

During my time in seminary, I wrestled with what biblical literalism does to the lives (read: minds, hearts, actions) of those who do not interrogate its roots. Simply put, biblical literalism is the belief that the Bible is the factual and literal word of God. As I dove deeper into theological study and doing ministry in my church field education placement, I began to reconcile the best approach to handling people whose faith was wrapped up in traditional ways of reading biblical texts. I also realized that God could hold the fullness of who I was and show me the way to keep my faith both intact *and* critically engaged with the evolving world before me. Leaving biblical literalism behind did not mean I had to leave the faith behind too. Instead, it was an invitation to claim a more robust faith as a sacred belonging that would grow with me and grace me with new ways of seeing and being with the world.

Seminary was also the time and place where I was introduced to womanist theology* (terms with an asterisk are also defined in the glossary) by religious scholars Rev. Dr. Emilie Townes and Dr. Stacey M. Floyd-Thomas, both of whom I took classes under while in seminary. Womanist theology reconsiders and revises traditions, practices, scriptures, and biblical interpretation with the specific purpose to empower and liberate Black women. It is an outgrowth of womanism,* introduced by Alice Walker in her 1983 book *In Search of Our Mothers' Gardens* as a social theory dedicated to unearthing the deeply rooted racial and gender-based oppression faced by Black women. Walker also offered womanism as a socio-historical critique of feminism, which tended to cater to the needs of white women and erase conversations regarding class and race. Therefore, womanism emphasizes the unique experiences of Black women and focuses on the intersections of race, gender, class, and sexuality.

Hallmarks of womanism include community and family, the relationships and healing found in the experiences of Black women, and a holistic approach to spirituality and communal thriving. Where feminism was too narrowly focused, womanism took Black feminism a step further and focused on uplifting all marginalized people—not just Black women. After Walker published her book, scholars like the late Rev. Dr. Katie Geneva Cannon, Dr. Jacquelyn Grant, and Dr. Delores S. Williams built on her framework. They applied womanist principles to Christian theology and disrupted the male-dominated Black theology and liberation movements.

With its focus on the holistic well-being of Black women and their communities, womanism continues to manifest in contemporary movements, initiatives, and cultural expressions. Present-day examples include the Black Lives Matter (BLM) movement, cofounded by Alicia Garza, Patrisse Cullors, and Opal Tometi, which embodies womanist principles by centering the experiences of Black people, particularly women and queer folks, in its fight against systemic racism and police violence. Social media platforms like Black Girls Rock! and hashtags like #BlackGirlMagic celebrate and affirm the beauty, strength, and achievements of Black women and girls, fostering a sense of community and empowerment. And organizations like SisterSong Women of Color Reproductive Justice Collective work to protect the reproductive rights of women of color. Their approach goes beyond pro-choice, advocating for the right to have children, not have children, and parent in safe and healthy environments. These examples show that womanism is not just a theoretical framework but a living, evolving movement that influences various aspects of contemporary culture, activism, and community building, always with a focus on the experiences and leadership of Black women.

Womanist theology, meanwhile, translates womanism into four tenets that mirror Walker's original definition (which you can find in the glossary). These four tenets—radical subjectivity, traditional communalism, redemptive self-love, and critical engagement—provide a framework for understanding and navigating the prescient theological, ethical, spiritual, and social concerns of Black women (don't worry—we'll talk more about these tenets when you join me later on the porch). I cannot begin to underscore how deeply personal womanist theology has been for me and so many others. Womanist theology gave me language for my (un)becoming and tools to articulate a more informed faith that took seriously the ways in which oppression, white supremacy, misogyny, homophobia, and other social ills had infiltrated the church. Womanist theology grew me up and graced me with the belief that I could begin again and face the "former pastors" of the world—not with violence but with the truth of vindication. It gave me confidence as I went from deconstructor to doubter (in the sense that deep questions and uncertainty became hallmarks of my faith) to re-memberer to relisher and back again. Simply put, womanist theology became a sacred belonging for me. And for this reason, I am honored to use it as a guiding and organizing framework to journey alongside you and provide you with tools and language to find yourself and your faith again.

Losing, stretching, or having your faith damaged doesn't always feel good. Yet goodness can come from it. After I finished seminary, I continued doing ministry under an amazing woman pastor, Rev. Dr. Judy D. Cummings, and was ordained at New Covenant Christian Church (Disciples of Christ). Within five years of my profession of ministry to my former pastor, God had moved swiftly and decidedly—taking me to a place where I could see what was denied as a reality for me: a woman pastor who would affirm me, nurture me, and ordain me into full-time ministry. A sacred belonging, indeed.

That is what has brought me here today. A clear calling to minister to those of you who are wrestling, even now, with whatever it is God is asking of you. A clear calling to speak to those of you who feel like you are on the margins and have no soft place to lay your head. A clear calling to walk with you as you fight for a faith that will fight for you and side with the oppressed. You know how in the Catholic tradition, the woman who is the head of the convent and shepherds the postulates and nuns is referred to as Reverend Mother? (Shout-out to the most notable Reverend Mothers in my millennial memory: Mother Teresa, Reverend Mother in the *Sound of Music*, and Reverend Mother in *Sister Act*, aka Minerva McGonagall in *Harry Potter*.) I want you to think of me as Reverend Auntie, or just plain Auntie will do. You are my adopted kin, my nieces, nephews, niblings—a flock of people I see as a sacred belonging and will love on and pour into the same way I care for my biological family members.

We should probably have a word about Aunties. It might help if I start with a poem I wrote a few years back about the proverbial Auntie as the force she is.

on everything—
Aunties be knowin'
a little something about everything.
about life.
about loss.
about love.
about lust.
about laughter.
about everything.

and in between knowin' all the things
she still be making time
to show up carrying the plate she cooked.
to be your secret carrier.
to care for the parts of you don't nobody else care for.
to carpool your stuff.
that you couldn't carry
because she got room
for everything.

like somewhere—
on her way to womanhood,
she learned how to be everywhere,
everytime,
and how to say all the names of everyone
you would ever be.
all because you call her Auntie.
and that's her everything.[1]

Aunties—particularly Black Aunties—play an indispensable role for the rearing of children. Historically, "Auntie" was a name bestowed upon Black women enslaved on plantations who were forced to take care of slave-owners' children. As time progressed and Black people were emancipated from chattel slavery, many Black women remained as domestic workers and caretakers in white people's homes. The "Auntie" moniker persisted, carrying with it a racial and gender stereotype of the ever sacrificial "Mammy" figure who would often raise white children of no kin to her while struggling to provide for the Black children she birthed.

What is important to note about this historical era of "Auntie-dom" is that many hallmarks of modern-day Auntie culture still feature elements of Aunties' resilience and resourcefulness at the height of segregation and oppression. The ways Aunt Sarah and Aunt Mae learned to feed multitudes with minimal food or scrape together a dollar out of fifteen cents became cultural wisdom passed down to us millennial Aunties who were raised with them as elders. And would-be / future Aunties like me took those lessons and added them to the formal educations (that they had busted their behinds to make sure) we got. And just like that (*snaps my fingers*), their wisdom and our wit became a noticeable, and powerful, cultural phenomenon that people—Black and non-Black alike—began to take great pride in.

Take, for instance, the moment when actor Michael B. Jordan greeted Angela Bassett on the 2023 Oscars stage with a simple line, "Hey, Auntie," after she lost the award for Best Supporting Actress. While some people may have thought he was only reenacting a line from their recent movie *Black Panther*, those of us learned in both Black and Auntie culture knew. He was speaking to the essence of what it means to respect and honor elder Black women who have done all they can, given their best, and shown us the way—only to come up short when it's time for a much-deserved award.

In that moment, Michael B. Jordan provided a glimpse of the true power of Auntie culture. Auntie culture connects us to people beyond biological ties and compels us toward loving relationships and protective bonds. I can attest that while I only have two aunts biologically, I have ten times that number of Aunties who were given to me because of their kinship with my parents or whom I adopted or cultivated a relationship with on my own.

It is not trivial or a marketing ploy to place Auntie as such a central figure to this book. Just as my poem says, Aunties *been* knowing who we were and saving our lives when we forgot. Aunties are basically the cooler versions of our parents because they come with all the same wisdom and none (or maybe I should just say less) of the condemnation. Aunties are, for many of us, the very people who show us what it *feels* like to experience sacred belonging. Because to them, you are among their most prized possessions—a sacred belonging gifted straight from God. And like Jesus, sent to us as God's sacred belonging, Aunties walk with, love on, and even heal every part of you. Especially the parts of you that others don't always see.

This is the essence of why Auntie is vital to this conversation. Because as much as we feel safe and seen and whole in their presence, we must fight to have that in ourselves, our relationship with God, and definitely in our faith spaces—whether formal or informal. You should be able to keep the same energy in your relationship with your faith like you have when you are excited to sit on the porch and talk with Auntie about your day, your dreams, or your doubts.

That's where I come in: your favorite Reverend Auntie (you following me on social media yet?). I have written letters to various audiences, Auntie-pistles to you, much like the apostle Paul wrote to specific communities and churches. There's a letter to my "hardheads"—folks who learn things the hard way. There's one to my "love-makers"—people stereotyped as promiscuous but who are truly just self-possessed. There's a letter for Gen Zers and another for boomers. There is something, hopefully, for everyone. And in the same way you can read the epistles in the Bible and glean something for your own life—even when those letters were meant for a different people in a different time—I believe you can read each letter in this book and be blessed by it.

Each Auntie-pistle includes a story (parable) from my personal narrative and practical methods to shift your theological perspective and faith expression. Auntie has gone the extra step in making sure you don't just learn from my own experiences. I've included prayers and prompts, including fill-in-the-blank writuals, for you to answer on your own and begin to put flesh on the bones of what you learn. Because, first of all, you ain't gonna make me do all the work. And second, I love you just that much to assign you homework. Trust me, it will all help in the long run.

I've touched briefly on womanist theology and its four tenets: radical subjectivity, traditional communalism, redemptive self-love, and critical engagement. In these pages, we'll consider how these manifest in sacred belonging. For anyone who desires to develop a more robust spirituality, we'll explore four belief statements, or theological commitments, that can help make womanist theology applicable and accessible for faith practice.

1. Truth-telling is spiritual discernment—Seeing and speaking truth (to power) is a necessary form of faith expression and Christian witness. It affirms the vital nature of God-given agency to change or impact our surroundings—particularly, in instances of oppression and unfairness.

2. Tribe is sanctuary—The intentionality with which we choose to build our chosen family or village of support oftentimes results in life-giving, life-affirming relationships akin to divine places of safety. This theological commitment is to live into the call to be(come) sources of refuge for oneself and others who otherwise would not experience care, inclusion, or welcome.

3. Tears are salvific work—This commitment is to lay hold of the vulnerability that liberates us from all forms of self-harm and deprecation and invites us into the deep healing work necessitated by disrupting pain, silence, and trauma. It is the ability to allow weeping and other forms of lament to usher us into a radical acceptance of self.

4. Transfiguration is social healing—This theological commitment is to accept the communal aspect of our faith over and against a Westernized notion of individual salvation unconcerned with the well-being of others. It is the invitation *do justice, love mercy, and walk humbly with God* as a reasonable act of service in tearing down the strongholds of oppression (white supremacy, sexism, misogyny, homophobia, transphobia, xenophobia,

Christian nationalism, ableism, etc.) as a form of spiritual warfare within us and in our own community.

The Auntie-pistles in this book are organized according to these four theological commitments of sacred belonging. After we get through each set of letters, you're invited up on the porch for tea and testimony about truth-telling, tribe, tears, and transfiguration. We'll also talk about how to engage sacred belonging through Scripture and other wisdom as found in Black women's sacred texts and stories. (You'll also find a glossary of terms at the back of the book to help as you navigate this new theological terrain.)

I pray that these Auntie-pistles and porch talk testimonials help you shift your theological perspective and faith expression. Together, we will work on reclaiming, recovering, or perhaps reifying your faith—and mine too. Because every time I share a bit about my own journey with someone else, I am reminded of the tender places in my faith that still need a little bit more tending.

If you're still with me, clearly you must wanna be here. So, consider me your new favorite Auntie (that makes us family now). Then take a deep breath and consider these words:

My faith is a sacred belonging.
A gift that makes room for who I am becoming.
A gift that I do not own alone but that welcomes my
    ownership of the co-journey.
I am worthy of experiencing sacred belonging.
A place where, when I am *still* enough, I hear God's voice
    saying: you are still *enough*.
Regardless of what has tried to kill me and has failed.[2]

We are a sacred belonging.

To a Creator who can handle all of who we are and who we are not.

May we find and create the sacred belonging.

That will heal us from the ills that try to make us believe we do not belong together.

SACRED BELONGING COMMITMENT #1

Truth-Telling Is Spiritual Discernment

"Do not think that in the king's palace you will escape any more than all the other Jews. For if you keep silent at this time, relief and deliverance will rise for the Jews from another place, but you and your father's family will perish. Who knows? Perhaps you have come to royal dignity for just such a time as this." Then Esther said in reply to Mordecai, "Go, gather all the Jews . . . and hold a fast on my behalf. . . . I will go to the king, though it is against the law, and if I perish, I perish."

—Esther 4:13–16

Beloved, sometimes you just have to call a thing a thing.
—Auntie Iyanla Vanzant

ONE

To My Too Growns

(People Who Have Sage Wisdom and Smart Mouths)

A PARABLE FOR MY TOO GROWNS

I grew up in the nineties. Yes, yes. It is true. I am a geriatric millennial. But be clear: I am part of the bridge generation. The group of kids who grew up in the advent of technology like the Nintendo and Game Boy and the rise of BET and MTV when music videos were still a thing. Likewise, given that cell phones and social media hadn't completely changed the way we do life (yet), I spent a great deal of time with my grandparents growing up. For weeks at a time, my older brother and I would go to Greenwood, Mississippi, and stay with my grandma and granddaddy during summer and holiday breaks. I'd say we got the best of both worlds—getting the privilege to experience the boom of the digital/techno age and sitting in the slow and steady wisdom of our elders.

I also grew up in a problematically (or predominantly) white small town in Arkansas and happened to be the only Black kid in many of my classes in elementary school. The constant feedback and remark I'd receive on my report cards was: "talks too much." Apparently, white teachers didn't have a lot of patience for an overly precocious and loquacious little Black girl. So, they tried to punish me into submission. I'd get my name written on the board for talking excessively in class. Year after year, teachers would move my desk around in class to prevent me from talking to my peers. One teacher even moved my desk directly in front of hers so that I'd be less inclined to talk. Baby, what she didn't know is that I was just gonna talk to her instead! And talk to her I did!

It did not matter what they tried to stop me from talking, I got my word count in for the day—*every day*. I laugh about it now. Funnily enough, when I was ordained a few years back, my grandmother stood up in front of the *entire* church and said: "My granddaughter was always an aggressive little girl." She said this as she explained I always stood up for what I believed and had no problem speaking my mind.

I think partly she might have been referring to one summer I spent with her and my granddaddy. It was around 1998 or so. I would've been a teenager then. And, true to form, I spent the day watching *60 Minutes*, CNN, and John Hagee because my grandfather refused to let anyone else change the channel even though he was sleep-watching the television. On this particular day, I was helping my grandmother sweep and vacuum in the living room while she did other housework elsewhere. My grandfather had gotten tripped up on one of the plastic mats that adorned their living room floor, and he wanted my grandma to come help him right that moment. (My grandfather was partially blind because of cat-aracts—so he required a lot of assistance.) Rather than wait patiently for her to come, he began hollering like someone was flogging him to death. In a not-so-nice-or-loving tone, he demanded her to come immediately.

I don't remember what exactly he said, but my grand-mother hollered back and told him she was coming as fast as she could. And I could hear the pain and annoyance in her voice. Well, that was all I needed to speak up too. "Grandaddy, you don't have to talk to her like that! She does all she can to take care of you and you're being mean. You should be grate-ful." That was all I could muster to say through my frustra-tion and fear. I was so angry that he would fix his mouth to speak to my grandmother that way after all she did to keep their household running. But I was also extremely scared that my grandmother would whup me for "talkin' back" and being disrespectful in their home. Still, I wasn't going to sit back and let nobody talk crazy to my grandma. Not even my granddaddy. So, in my Queen Esther moment, I said to myself, "If I perish, I perish." And spoke up anyway.

Turns out, I did not get a whupping or even a reprimand from my grandmother. Even better, my grandfather soft-ened toward my grandmother and was noticeably less agi-tated and more gracious for the rest of the day. I do not take credit for that moment of grace I believe my grandmother needed, because I *know* something beyond me accompa-nied and empowered me to speak boldly. Normally, that little unctioning to be aggressive and speak out is some-thing that gets a bad rap when it takes residence in Black girls. And its commonplace for Black youth and teens to be accused of being "too grown" if we get out of line or break ranks with the social norm of children keeping silent when adults are present.

But what always baffled me about this expectation is that I was encouraged and pushed to be a leader in everywhere else but my family's home. I was raised and socialized to be extremely thoughtful, well-spoken, and mature from a very young age. From the time I could talk, my mom had me in church—reciting Easter speeches, participating in Christmas plays, you name it. At school, the same expectation was clear: always stand up for what is right and never be swayed by the crowd. Yet here I was, almost deathly afraid to use my voice in the place where I should've felt the safest to do so.

We have to be careful enough to interrogate the ways we rear children, particularly Black girls. We live in a time and culture where children are adultified, sexualized, or punished for reaching puberty too soon. At the same time, we demonize youth who are able to express themselves, characterizing them as disrespectful or having a smart mouth far before we affirm them as fierce and future leaders. Which one is it? What attribute do we want from them? Do we want them to be mature enough to speak up about things that bother them? Or do we want them to be silent just because an adult said so? Do we want them to know the beauty of having a sense of autonomy and choice over their own bodies? Or do we want them to acquiesce and consent to maltreatment because we've taken away their voice?

I believe this silencing of our own courage and numbing our propensity for speaking the truth begins in childhood. Consequently, our capacity for censoring our voice spills over into our faith relationships well into adulthood. And as a result, we are unable to allow ourselves room to say the quiet parts out loud when it comes to things that don't make sense in the Bible or our faith spaces. Why can't we put voice to the things found in Scripture that trouble us? For example, what does it mean that Hagar conceived Ishmael after she was forced to reproduce with Abraham? Why do so many of the sacred texts of the Bible have to refer to sinful nations as prostitutes or harlots? That we—particularly, women—are somehow not allowed or empowered to say these things in the very spaces where we should feel safe enough to discuss them (our faith spaces) seems like a sad waste of space to me. Growing up, it was tortuous to walk the fine line of silencing myself in the presence of adults and authority figures while navigating when it was appropriate to speak up and be the leader I was taught to be. It seems appropriate, then, for me to call out the cognitive dissonance that is preventing too many people from pursuing a deeper, more curious faith life.

The implications of this suppression are as sad as they are enraging. But I am most concerned with how it teaches little girls (who turn into grownups) to simply turn their brains off when they go to church and any other place where they are not empowered. I am very thankful for the seeds of boldness that were watered within me as a girl. And many of my boss-sista-friends feel the same. Though we were labeled as too grown, too bossy, too whatever (and many times, got in trouble for it), we are all now leaders or trailblazers in our respective fields. And truth-telling is the main characteristic, or common thread, that each of us preserved—no matter how difficult—through our childhoods and now prize as adults in our professional roles.

Truth-telling, which I offer as the first commitment of sacred belonging*, means speaking truth to power. It embodies both the holy courage to stand boldly declaring life in the face of death and a defiant posture of audacious belief in a better, higher way. Truth-telling is the outward sign of spiritual discernment, which gives us the ability to see the wrong that is, many times, invisible to others, and to call for it to be made right. And truth-telling is a step toward sacred belonging. It is a guiding principle that invites courageous curiosity that enables you to radically transform your relationship with what you believe about God and the powers that be. Truth-telling allows us to resist harmful ideologies and claim the agency necessary to pursue liberation and wholeness. Auntie translation: Truth-telling is a superpower that helps you call a thing a thing (meet me on the porch for more on this later).

If you are silent about your pain, they will kill you and say you enjoyed it.
　　　　—Zora Neale Hurston, *Their Eyes Were Watching God*

A PRAYER FOR MY TOO GROWNS

　　God who gives us holy courage,
　　we praise You for giving us a spirit of boldness
　　that empowers us to discern the truth and speak it forth.
　　We thank You for watering the seeds of defiance
　　that grow up in us and shout freedom in our voice.
　　Help us, oh God, to cultivate that courage
　　to ask hard questions, say hard things, and strive even
　　　　harder.
　　And make sure that our silence is not choking the life
　　　　from someone in our midst.

Show us the way to tell the truth, even if our voice
   shakes.
And keep us on the path toward reconciling
that which no longer serves us
and the faith anew that will save us
from darkness, death, and despair.
Give us wisdom to bear witness
to our own sacred belonging,
so that we will find urgency
in creating safe spaces for those around us.
Amen and ashé.[1]

A PROMPT FOR MY TOO GROWNS
welcome

- What have you been taught, since childhood, about truth-telling—particularly, in the form of protest or advocacy?

- How has truth-telling been characterized (or demonized) as being an agitator or troublemaking, and what is the consequence of this for the truth-teller? Think about present-day, public examples of this.

- When have you felt the need to silence your truth, or someone else's, to keep peace with your family or with people in places you frequent?

- What might be at stake (socially, spiritually, culturally, politically) if you invite truth-telling into your faith or faith-spaces?

witness

> I have seen how unspoken rules cause you to edit your-
> self in the moment.
>
> How you hold your tongue or your hands so that you do
> not stumble over your words or work.
>
> But bending yourself to fit into a box of safety is no lon-
> ger serving you.
>
> And has only made you comfortable with being small.
>
> I pray that you will know the relief of stretching your
> cramped limbs toward liberation.
>
> And that the joints of your soul will release the stiffness
> required of silence.
>
> For you deserve to bask in freedom just as uncontained
> water flows.
>
> Unbothered and undeterred by the terrain underneath
> you.
>
> I hope I get to witness the way liberation looks on you.
>
> —love, Auntie.

writual

In the Christian faith, we perform litanies as a call-and-re-
sponse within a religious community. Rituals such as litanies connect us with our faith beliefs and the neighbors with
whom we recite each theological statement. The writuals in
this book offer a space for you to think introspectively about
what God is calling you to do and the witnesses you want to
accompany you on your journey of sacred belonging. Please
fill in the blanks with whatever seems right and befitting
for you. Then practice saying it aloud or in the presence of
trusted friends and loved ones who support you.

The call: I will know the _____ (noun meaning strength) of truth-telling even when I am _____ (phrase that means scared or hesitant). I will _____ (word that means a form of expression) the truth, in love and liberation so that I may experience _____ (a phrase referring to sacred belonging) that I have yet to experience for myself. I will ask God to awaken me to the realities before me that need my attention, and I commit to _____ (phrase meaning "call out") the harm. I release myself from performative silence because I accept _____ (describe what you want to own as an emerging truth-teller), and that other people's lives are connected to my ability to try. I will no longer allow the fear of opening my mouth to stop me from using the _____ (noun meaning strength) of my voice.

The response: I/we stand in agreement with who you are becoming. And with God as our witness, we are delighted to welcome your bravery as you strive to exercise spiritual discernment as truth-telling so that others around you are inspired to do the same.

TWO

To My Hardheads

(People Who Typically Learn the Hard Way)

A PARABLE FOR MY HARDHEADS

In Black culture, a commonly held belief and proverb says, "A hard head will make a soft [behind]." In other words, those who are typically stubborn and do things the hard way are more likely to be on the receiving end of corporal punishments (also known as whuppings or spankings). A nicer way to put it, if you will, is that life lessons are the best teachers.

I grew up hearing this statement frequently. Not because I was hardheaded or disobedient (no, I'd never do that). But simply as a reinforcement that if you stepped out of line, my parents and elders reserved the right to lovingly beat the brakes off you. To be clear, neither of my parents ever resorted to that kind of violence with my brother or me. However, both of us certainly received our fair share of whuppings—which, to this day, neither of my parents regret. After all (and they always quote), Proverbs 13:24 teaches that to "spare the rod is to spoil the child."

I am not sure where I fall on the spectrum of gentle parenting and old-school parenting, but I have started to question forms of punishment that include physically laying hands on a child. I find myself teetering between popping my two-year-old on the hand for her displays of disobedience and instantly feeling remorse or regret. Other times, I find it is the only way to get a proper response (read: submission) to what I need her to do in that very moment. The conundrum is always difficult to navigate.

Beyond my own personal feelings about hard heads making soft behinds, it would not be very Auntie of me if I didn't offer more nuance about the other social implications of whuppings as punishment. From the origins of the transatlantic slave trade, colonizers and enslavers developed tactics for keeping enslaved persons in check and on the plantation. Subservience was demanded through physical suffering. At the 1995 Million Man March, organizer Louis Farrakhan read excerpts from a speech known as the Willie Lynch letter, which was supposedly recorded in the eighteenth century for the purposes of breaking Black men and women and enslaving them. Though the Lynch letter has since been debunked as a hoax, its violent and oppressive rhetoric was virulent. It premised that physical violence against Black bodies is the only way to control enslaved people. And this is something that still rests in the psyches of many Black people descended from formerly enslaved persons in the United States.

My mother and father have always demanded respect from their children. Having grown up in segregated Mississippi in the 1960s, they knew too well what happened to Black children who did not know the rules of engagement. You had to say *ma'am* and *sir* to white people. You had to move to the other side of the street or off the sidewalk if white people approached. You rode on the back of the bus. You went around back to get food from restaurants. You drank at separate water fountains labeled "coloreds only." And you most certainly did not make any sudden movements or appear aggressive when in the presence of police officers. You behaved respectably and politely. The end, no other options. The vestiges of white supremacy* demanded compliance with these rules. The tactics used to get it were rooted in physical forms of punishment.

I think that's why "hardheaded" children were viewed as problems and the recipients of such vitriolic anger from parents and grandparents and guardians. Because underneath that anger was fear. A collective memory of trauma and suffering that reminded them that their loved ones could be snatched or taken away if they did not do as "master" said. If that is the case, then "a hard head makes a soft behind" is a sad but necessary reality. It's an admission that whupping children is an act of desperation to survive an oppressive regime that you have no idea how to resist or confront to keep your children safe.

Assata Shakur (aunt of the late rapper Tupac Shakur), an author and political activist who trained with the Black Panther Party and joined the Black Liberation Army, remains a pivotal figure of the Black Power movement of the late 1970s. "I hate war, and I hate having to struggle," she said while talking about the person she'd become because of such oppressive regimes.

> I wish I had been born into a world where it was unnec-essary. This context of struggle and being a warrior and being a struggler has been forced on me by oppression. Otherwise, I would be a sculptor, or a gardener, carpen-ter—You know, I would be free to be so much more . . . I guess part of me or a part of who I am, a part of what I do is being a warrior—a reluctant warrior, a reluctant strug-gler. But I do it, because I'm committed to life.[1]

As someone who often wonders what else I could be if I didn't have to be so strong all the time, so much of her statement resonates with me. Some of us learn how to be hardheads because there just isn't anything else to be. But should that mean that we should also be so used to suffering that we expect it? If the saying holds true, then we should all become perpetual martyrs.

At the risk of boring you to death but in the hopes of making this more clear, let me offer a personal story. From when I was about age six to age eight, my mother scraped together her single-mom coins and enrolled me in dance school. Though I enjoyed getting the nice, frilly costumes and performing, I was not the best ballerina. You see, I took my frame and height from my father, who is extremely tall (six foot seven, to be exact) and athletic. While I had the height to be an amazing dancer, I did not have the gracefulness. I was flat-footed where I should have been pointy-toed. I was too powerful where I should have been demure. I was, in all fairness, tomboyish when I should have been more feminine (whatever that means). In short, I was just too hard when I needed to be soft.

I couldn't *learn* the softness they wanted me to embody. Sharp elbows, pointy knees, and a loud voice had already claimed for me a life of more aggressive sports like basketball and volleyball where you had to attack and take up space. I didn't see how to be anything else. I think a lot of us suffer from a similar lack of imagination or vision. Whether because of oppressive forces or life circumstances, we develop calluses in the form of prickly personalities and defense mechanisms. And we begin to put on armor and become *reluctant warriors* who relish being hard because we don't know to be soft. We do things alone or in isolation because we don't know how to ask for help. We cling to brute force because receiving soft-ness might break us apart. But today, we're gonna get free of all that mess. Or as my granny used to say: We will tell the truth and shame the devil!

Telling the truth (and, yes, shaming the devil) means we name our disembodied, dysfunctional behavior—behavior like the normalization of toxic productivity over personal wellness or requiring people to remain silent about things that are causing harm—as by-products of a sin-riddled world where a web of oppression has forced us to become robots feeding the machine. (Yes, I think capitalism is a huge culprit here, and I don't mind calling it the devil that it is.) Telling the truth means we are honest about how much we are carrying and how heavy is this crown of thorns that is required of living so self-sacrificially all the time. Telling the truth means we push against the narratives that make it easy to believe that white women are worthy of rest and care and Black women and other women of color are subject to being over-labored and uncared for. Telling the truth about being hardheads means we begin to open our hearts and ask our-selves the hard but necessary questions.

Questions that will help us get to the root of why and when we became so closed off and closed-minded. Questions that will help us identify the places where our first response would be violence instead of empathy. Questions that will help us determine where we abandoned ourselves desperately reach-ing for what we thought, or were told, we were supposed to be. Questions like Peter asked in Matthew 17:1–8 when he was up on the mountain praying with James, John, and Jesus. A few days earlier, Jesus had told the disciples he would suffer and die. He prophesied that some of them would see the Son of Man coming into the glory of the kin-dom.* And while they were on the mountain, Jesus' appearance suddenly shifted to a bright and glorious presence. As Jesus was trans-figured before them, Peter said "Lord, it is good for us to be here. If you wish, I will set up three tents. . ." His statement began in certainty and ended in a proposition for Peter to busy himself in an act of service. In other words, Peter was like *Lord, this is awesome—but what you want me to do now?*

At face value, this seems like a proper response. Peter didn't wanna seem derelict in his servant duties during this holy moment, right? But let Auntie help y'all out a little with some prophetic imagination. Most of us are so accustomed to allowing Jesus to show up only as a suffering servant in our lives because we believe servitude to be our only portion. When, in contradistinction, Jesus shows up in the razzle-dazzle of all His glory, we don't know what to do, because we have no idea how to sit in or with goodness. Peter's inferred question "Lord, this is good for us to be here. . . but what should we do with this goodness?" should be an invitation for us to ask the same—with a slight variation.

What would it mean for us to say: Lord, is it okay if I sit here in this goodness with you? Lord, is it all right if I stay in this grace-filled spaciousness with you for a while? Lord, can I be in the presence of the light of Your softness for as long as You would allow? Lord, I don't want to be so hardheaded anymore; might You touch me so I am no longer afraid of what's on the other side of this mountain? For it is in the asking that God will reveal that hardhead means we are that much easier to love.

A PRAYER FOR MY HARDHEADS

God who hears our questions and honors our quietude,
we are grateful that You relentlessly pursue us even when
  we are unprepared to receive You.
Help us, oh God, to be mindful of our jagged edges and
  wearied souls.
We run ourselves ragged because we are scared of asking
  for help or stopping for respite.
Remind us, Lord, that there is no reward for pushing
  ourselves to the brink of our capacity.
Strengthen us to lay down the burdens which do not
  belong to us—even if they are labels given to us by
  someone else.
And give us wisdom to speak the truth, in love, about
  what we desire and who we want to be.
Thank You for all the ways You blessed us with
  self-determination.
Now, give us eyes to see ourselves as delicate and worthy
  of support—

as sacred belongings with hard heads and soft hearts.
Amen and ashé.

A PROMPT FOR MY HARDHEADS
welcome

- Identify some hardheaded people in your life. What other adjectives would you use to describe them?

- What is the truth that you—or other hardheads—need to hear to be liberated from isolation or obstinance?

- When have you resorted to violence or a lack of empathy because you saw no avenue for softness?

- What would it take for you to view (and receive) softness as a sacred belonging? If this question causes you discomfort, why do you think that is so?

witness

I have seen how you've learned to carry more than your fair share.
I notice the calluses that have formed on your hands and around your heart.
And I know you believe your capacity to bear many loads makes you strong.
Hear me gently say: You will know your true strength when you learn to put down that which does not belong to you.
You deserve to know leisure and laughter, celebration and softness.
I believe that labor is not your only portion.
I hope I get to witness you walking in that place of lightness.
—love, Auntie.

writual

The call: I will embrace the _____ (noun meaning magnitude or essence) of telling the truth about the hard stuff because I want to _____ (phrase that means release) myself from carrying that burden. I will _____ (word that means to communicate or uncover) what I need and accept _____ (word or phrase meaning support) so that I may _____ (a phrase referring to enjoyment) a sense of sacred belonging that I long to experience for myself. I will ask God to _____ (verb or phrase meaning to show) me how to belong to myself before I belong to limitless responsibilities required of me. I release negative associations or beliefs I once held about softness because I understand _____

_____

(describe what you now know to be false about softness) and that I am allowed to have it for myself. I will live into my soft era and strive to show others the way to their own softness because _____ (a phrase explaining why others deserve to be gifted with that truth).

The response: I/we stand in agreement with who you are becoming. And with God as our witness, we are delighted to welcome your bravery as you strive to exercise spiritual discernment as truth-telling so that others around you are inspired to do the same.

THREE

To My Holy Rollers

(People Struggling with Unhealthy Theological Ties)

A PARABLE FOR MY HOLY ROLLERS

The passing of religious giant Bishop Carlton Pearson in 2023 has me questioning a lot these days. Especially because his reputation for the "gospel of inclusion" preceded him and painted his legacy in shame and infamy rather than support and, well, inclusion. (Take this as your sign to watch the movie *Come Sunday*.) As he departed staunch evangelical beliefs of hell and shifted his views on salvation through Jesus, many of his former supporters distanced themselves and left his church. Others denounced him as a heretic. This was a man who had dedicated his life to the ministry and spearheaded the Azusa revival movement, a huge gathering year over year where people accepted Christ, healing, and being part of a beloved community.* If there ever was anyone viewed as a sacred belonging to the body of believers, it should have been Bishop Pearson.

Yet so many self-professed holy rollers treated him like an unclean pariah who had no business even uttering the name Jesus. Simply because they were certain that he was in need of repentance and that they were righteous in their own beliefs. Somehow, he became expendable as long as their doctrine remained the most important thing. I've never been cast out of my faith community in such a manner. But I have become an outsider at the very church I loved because of doctrinal differences and theological beliefs. And I can tell you this much: it's painful.

As I shared earlier, I too went through a painful journey of unlearning toxic theologies that threatened to keep me from God's truth and my destiny. After going to school in Colorado for a master's in electrical engineering, I returned home to Arkansas and to the church I grew up in. A few years before my return, the church had gone through major upheavals, and many members had left the church. That meant several of the ministries were suffering, and as a result, the youth ministry was nearly nonexistent. Because I'd spent my time in Colorado developing a youth ministry for the small non-denominational church I attended there, I volunteered to help my home church get the youth involved again. I went to work creating Bible studies, planning youth lock-ins and immersion trips, and starting a step team that performed at churches across the city. It was a fun and vibrant time in the life of the church.

About a year into serving as the unofficial youth director, I began to sense a discomfort that I couldn't describe. It wasn't that we didn't have good participation or that I didn't enjoy the kids. That part was flourishing more than ever. But something felt . . . off. I endured many sleepless nights during that season. I would cry out to God in prayer, begging to understand the longing in my soul that I just couldn't quench. And one night, after a friend had spoken a word of encouragement to me, God affirmed what my friend had said and led me to several scriptures about preaching the gospel. But even with this divine revelation, I had no idea how to respond to what appeared to be a calling from God. I'd been taught my entire life that women don't preach. What was God asking me to do? Why would God lead me to something that God prohibited for my gender? But maybe I was wrong. After all, I'd proven myself by serving the youth and the church faithfully. The testimonies of the children alone should've been enough to convince me. Yet I still needed (or wanted) external validation to reassure me that I'd heard God correctly.

So, I went to my pastor and told him about my call to ministry. And there on that ordinary day, in between the pews that I'd grown up on, he sat there looking me square in my face and told me I had not heard God. In fact, he pulled out a Bible from the back of one of those pews and walked me through nearly every New Testament text that had some mention of women remaining silent in the church (thanks, Paul and Timothy, your letters aged so well). I sat there humiliated. Listening in silence because that was literally the only thing I could think to do. I had no language to pull from and speak up on my behalf. As my pastor would always say, "God said it, that settled it."

I won't rehash everything you've already read. By this point, you know that day became the disruptive event that I needed to begin tending to my faith and my beliefs so that I could, indeed, understand what God was asking of me. And I left my home church. I bounced around a bit until I found myself enrolled in seminary. And there I began to develop the language, skills, and tools to respond to the theological questions that had riddled me ever since my pastor attempted to scare the truth out of me by reading scripture taken out of context and narrowly interpreted.

Other things began to happen, too. Beyond completely detaching myself from the biblical literalism that said that women have no business leading or preaching in the church, I also began to sit with the cringey elements of evangelical teachings that just did not make a lick of sense. Like, how in the world can you "love the sinner, but hate the sin" when talking about gay and transgender people? And why would God make me heterosexual but then allow someone else to "choose" to be gay? In the matter of Christian supremacy, how do we make sense of our theologies of "chosenness" when *nearly none of us are Jewish*? If we want to follow the line of biblical literalist thinking, last time I checked, most US-based Christians are Gentiles. And how do we reconcile how the displacement of people and colonization and occupation show up in biblical text and are *still* being justified in our present day?

We have to examine our insatiable need to draw boundaries around God's acceptance, grace, and love. What righteousness do we gain by insisting on the existence of hell when so many people are already living their own versions of hell (thanks to forms of oppression like economic disenfranchisement and an unfair healthcare system)? We are so bound up in needing to be right about doctrine that we miss out on the opportunity to love God and God's people. Now, hear Auntie, and hear me good. I am not saying that our faith beliefs should be a free-for-all where anything goes. I am simply suggesting that our faith should lead us to make room for our questions, our differences, and our struggles. The last thing our faith should do is leave people for dead. Rather, it should always leaven unto life.

I liken it to the teensy parable found in Matthew 13:33. On this beautiful day in the life of Jesus' teaching ministry, He is teaching the disciples about the parable of the sower and explaining why parables are His tool of choice to reveal things to them about the kin-dom of God. After interpreting the meaning of one parable, He tells them the parable of the yeast: "The [kin-dom] of heaven is like yeast that a woman took and mixed in with three measures of flour until all of it was leavened." What does this have to do with our faith expressions and theological beliefs? Well, I'm so glad you asked. Leaven, or yeast, works via a chemical process of decay to catalyze growth, which sets off a chain reaction, causing it to become a raising agent in any compound it's mixed in. Auntie's translation: leaven takes that which deals in death and raises it to life.

My mother is a prime example of the practical application of this life-giving principle. When I was in third grade, I had a not-so-nice teacher. I was the only Black kid in her class, and her disposition toward me suggested that I was a problem she did not want to solve with kindness or care. Instead, she was not only cold and crass toward me, but she also shamed me quite often for minor talking offenses (remember, I told y'all I was a talker). One day, we had spelling-bee practice. When it was my turn, she asked me to spell the word *already*. I knew how to spell that word, y'all. I was smart as a whip. Spelling *already* should have been light work. Only, it wasn't. I misspelled it by one letter, and the damage ensued, literally. "At the rate you're going," my teacher said—in front of the entire class—"you're never going to be able to spell." I was devastated. And a little bit of my spunk and spirit died that day.

But here's where the leaven enters the mix. Though I didn't tell my mom what had happened—nor had I voiced any concerns before that disastrous spelling-bee day—she'd been peeped that something wasn't right with me. Previous parent teacher conferences had alerted my mother's spidey senses that my teacher wasn't too fond of me. So as the school year wore on and she saw me becoming more withdrawn, she knew my teacher was the issue.

I can't remember how long it was after the spelling bee, but my mom showed up at the school one day and politely requested (sike!—more like demanded) a meeting with my principal and teacher. I don't know what was said in that closed-door session, but what I do know is that my mom checked me out of school early that day, took me to get a treat, and told me that my teacher wouldn't mess with me anymore. Like that little bit of leaven that the woman took and hid inside the flour, my mother showed up and hid a little leaven in me—raising me up and helping me breathe life again. Where I'd been suffering a silent death, she refused to let my teacher have the last say.

I don't think it's a stretch to stake the claim that our faith beliefs and theological commitments should never leave people for dead but should always leaven people to life. Yet, somehow, I find that many well-meaning, Jesus-loving Christians are so bound by rigid constructs of how to read the Bible or the binary debate between wrong or right that they write all these rules upon proverbial scrolls and wrap them into their hair like rollers adorning their crowns. In an effort to wrap themselves so tightly up in these rules, they often refuse to recognize the complex nature of humanity because "holiness" is all that matters. And thus, they shut their ears and silence voices speaking different truths from their own.

God, I'm so glad that my mother showed up, stood up, and spoke up on my behalf. When I didn't have the language or the tools to defend myself, she became like the woman with a little bit of leaven—laying all inhibition and appearances of "holiness" aside to come to my aide. She didn't follow protocol when it came to resurrecting me back to life. She did what the moment required of her. That began with a simple question: "How do I respond to what my gut is telling me?" And then she followed with speaking truth to power and setting a firm and lasting warning to my teacher who sought to dim my light. This leavening precedent would hide within me until it was reactivated after that disruptive encounter with my former pastor. Only this time, I would take that little bit of leaven and allow that death-dealing day to set off a chain reaction in my search for truth. And I found my voice in the process.

A PRAYER FOR MY HOLY ROLLERS

God who extends grace and new mercies,
we thank You for modeling the way to honor our
humanities,
and showing us the way to holiness is by humbly serving
others.
We ask that You show us how to transform death into life

so that our loved ones are leavened where they were once
left in despair.

Teach us, oh God, that our belief in You should not
require bruising.

For Jesus *already* spelled out the end of such suffering on
the cross.

Instead, make us treat everyone like the sacred belonging
they are—

even if it means we set our doctrines down to do so.

Amen and ashé.

A PROMPT FOR MY HOLY ROLLERS

welcome

- What is your definition of *holiness*, and how does it show
  up in the way you treat others?

- When have your faith beliefs (about holiness, hell, or
  otherwise) asked you to condemn or cast someone aside?
  When have they asked you to embrace or encourage
  someone?

- Where do you need to hide a little leaven in your life and
  relationships with others? What might the parable of the
  leaven teach you about sacred belonging**?**

witness

I have seen how "religious" rules cause you to contort
yourself and correct others.

I've watched how you hold on to rules like your life
depends on it.

But bending yourself to fit into a box of "holiness"
because it seems safe is no longer serving you.

And has only made you comfortable with making others
    small so that they fit in too.
I pray that you will release yourself from the grasp of
    closed-mindedness.
And that you absolve yourself from walking on the tight-
    rope of perfection.
For you deserve to be raised up like leaven.
And to activate others to rise up instead of shrink.
I pray I get to witness the beauty of this truth upon you.
                                —love, Auntie.

writual

The call: I will not allow the weight of death-dealing beliefs to
_____ (phrase meaning to force) me to stuff peo-
ple into boxes. I will, instead, _____ (verb meaning to act)
as a leavening agent to free myself and others from unnecessary performances of so-called "righteousness." I understand
that we are all _____ (phrase meaning beautiful)
parts of God's creation, deserving of life-affirming love and
care. And I will _____ (phrase meaning speak or
confirm) this truth even if it's unpopular or I am standing
alone.

The response: I/we stand in agreement with who you are
becoming. And with God as our witness, we are delighted
to welcome your bravery as you strive to exercise spiritual
discernment as truth-telling so that others around you are
inspired to do the same.

FOUR

To My Nephews

(All *Boys and Men*)

A PARABLE FOR MY NEPHEWS

My freshman year of college, I witnessed a near-cataclysmic event. It was the first big football game of the school year, and though it was foreign to me, people were pregaming in our dorm. At the time, I wasn't a drinker—I grew up in a strict religious household—so I had no idea that some college youth drank as much as what I was about to see. After the game was over and people began leaving to finish the night with munchies and a late-night movie in our rooms, we all went back to our dorm. That's when I and a couple of my friends noticed our hallmate essentially being carried by a host of fraternity boys. We happened to be joined by my best friend's group of guy friends from the neighboring HBCU (historically Black college/university). In case you aren't catching my drift, let me say it like this: here we were, a group of four Black freshmen girls with a group of five to seven freshmen Black guys, watching a throng of white guys carrying a lone and drunken white girl to her room. My anxiety is rising just recalling this story.

We quickly began whispering to one another, trying to see what we should say or do. *Girl, do you see that?* Followed by: *Yes, girl. Judy [not her real name] is drunk again—but who are those boys, and where they think they finna go?* That queued up the responses from our guy friends: *Nah, man, we can't let her go out like that, bruh. We don't know what them dudes gone do to her once they get her back to her room.* Our guy friends decided to take matters into their own hands. And they asked the frat boys where they were headed with Judy. To which the frat boys responded: "Don't worry about it. We belong here. But where are *y'all* going?" We all knew what they were insinuating—that this group of Black students couldn't possibly be attending such a prestigious university, thereby canceling our credibility in trying to make sure our classmate was okay.

Needless to say, the testosterone kicked in quickly and our guy friends stepped to the frat boys, demanding they let Judy go to her room accompanied by some of us (her hallmates). When the frat boys wouldn't comply, chaos broke loose. The frat boys got up in our guy friends' faces—and our friends were not the kind of people to back down. As most Black boys and males were raised, particularly in the South, there is a responsibility to stand up for and protect women in their midst. Once our guys saw how the frat boys pushed us women aside in the scuffle, it was all hands on deck. Thank goodness no punches were landed. Our resident advisor Shantay (also not her real name) showed up right as the frat boys were about to catch some hands. She instructed them to leave immediately, or she would call campus police. With much profanity and reluctance, the boys dropped Judy like a bad habit and left. As Shantay went to tend to Judy, who was completely passed out, we were left to deal with the aftermath of what had just happened.

Our guy friends were livid, of course, and they wanted to go after the frat boys. My best friend was crying and begging them to calm down and to stay put. A hallmate (another Black girl who had heard what was happening) came out of her room and began reciting the same statement to our guy friends over and over: "This is not a good idea, Black man. It won't end well for you if you leave here like this." *This is not a good idea, Black man. It won't end well for you if you leave like this, Black man.* Her words were simple, but they weighed a lot. And we all understood what she was saying. If campus police showed up and saw a group (read: angry mob) of Black men going to confront a group of white guys, no matter how shady and suspect the frat boys' behavior had been, the blame and suspicion would immediately fall on our friends. Her repeated stanza of the poem we didn't write but knew like the back of our hands finally broke through to the leader of our group of guy friends. And he got really quiet, though the anger was still pulsating from his body. He was seething, and it was palpable. And that memory has never left my body, even in the twenty years since it happened.

If only I had understood then what I know to be true now. You see, our guy friends bottled up their explosive rage—which surfaced as anger and aggression—because they did not know how to be vulnerable in that moment. At play underneath was the intersection of race and class and gender; a legacy that had poured into them the performance of patriarchy as a rite of passage to manhood and a means of survival for their loved ones. What they'd been taught, against this regime of anti-Blackness and misogyny* and white supremacy was that they could only ever be big, bad, angry Black men. And never scared young boys allowed to express sadness, disappointment, or fear.

Once all the bravado died down and the pure emotion subsided, I saw these guys sitting in the fullness of knowledge that what happened could've very well ended their lives, like our hallmate warned. And the dissonance that had to come from that was viscerally received and processed, though never voiced aloud. I think the guys likely struggled to ask themselves in the aftermath: When we show up for everyone else to protect them like we've been taught, who shows up for us? If all we are taught to be is protectors, how will we know how to be anything else? What I don't think any of our young minds recognized then is that we, the women, indeed showed up for them. Even through our tears and with our smaller frames, we stood as a barrier between those frat boys and our guys. Yet I don't think our friends would have seen our attempts as protection, because protection, to them, was supposed to be a masculine trait.

I tell this story to raise a necessary discussion about the ways we socialize or expect our nephews (or boys and men, more broadly) to behave when calamity strikes. I vividly remember the look of terror and trauma in our friends' eyes, yet the only way they could express their emotion was through anger and rage. What would it have taken for them to express pain or sorrow with a range of vulnerability that would allow them to hold space for their own tender places? This is the sad but predictable outcome of patriarchy—the systemic socialization of men to have a disproportionate power in social, economic, political, and religious institutions. Our nephews have little to no means to explore the fullness of who they can be without the expectation of a masculinity they did not define for themselves.

Black feminist scholar bell hooks said it far more eloquently than I can:

> The first act of violence that patriarchy demands of males is not violence toward women. Instead, patriarchy demands of all males that they engage in acts of psychic self-mutilation, that they kill off the emotional parts of themselves. If an individual is not successful in emotionally crippling himself, he can count on patriarchal men to enact rituals of power that will assault his self-esteem.[1]

We could all see the effects of such emotional debilitation on the pained faces of our friends, yet we had no means to free them of it. It was as if their internalized patriarchy was also ours—a burden to carry and stifle our emotion. Again, hooks gives us language to better understand patriarchy. "Patriarchy," she writes, "has no gender."[2] Even though some of its deepest impacts are felt by boys and men, patriarchy weighs all of us down.

Here is the truth I would speak on behalf of our guys—all our nephews—now that I've had twenty years to think about it and learn the language and skills necessary to articulate it: The hallmarks of white supremacy have only left crumbs of scarcity for you to feast upon as empty nourishment for your soul. You fear lack and losing control; therefore, you toughen up and hide any signs that you may be struggling. Behind all that is an all-consuming need for love and affection that you only know how to fill with the erotic and with pleasure. So you move back and forth between somatic extremes of infiltrating rage and intoxicating romance because you have numbed your ability to feel or experience anything in between. Thus, you perform masculinity as something you put on like a costume—cosplaying the roles prescribed to you about what it means to be a "real" man.

Yet there is so much more for you, for all of us. Because when you begin to fight for your personhood and vulnerability as a sacred belonging that has been denied to you, you unlock your true power. You deserve to frolic and skip. You deserve to laugh hysterically. You deserve to enjoy the warm embrace of all people—not just women. You deserve to know it's okay to cry, ask for help, or say you don't know. You deserve to resist the archetypes of the mandingo or sambo (these derogatory terms allude to a man's genitals or his ability to shuck and jive for white audiences), which cast you as a tool for pleasure or entertainment across multiple narratives you never wrote. You deserve to have men and non-men alike show up for you, hold space for you, and make room for *all* of you. You deserve dignity, joy, and peace. You deserve safe and soft spaces to land. And you deserve loving accountability to help you realize the fullness of your potential.

Maybe if we'd said those things that fateful night twenty years ago in our dorm, more of those guys would've gone on to be. Just *be*, no qualifier or achievement. Instead, a few of them dropped out of college, and I lost track of the rest. I do know that the most vocal leader of the group is doing well and has a family of his own now—a wife and two boys. I hope he reads this. And passes the message to his beautiful sons. As I understand it, one of them loves to dance. And not just hip-hop—but ballet, jazz, all of it (thank goodness he's more graceful than little Shantell was in her ballet days). In most Black churches, boys dancing on the liturgical dance team is still stigmatized or prohibited altogether. I hope that man reads this and continues to affirm his son(s) from a tender place. Just letting them be. And protecting them from the patriarchy that would do violence to them. The same way he protected us.

A PRAYER FOR MY NEPHEWS

God who is our protector,
we thank You for showing us the other side of
     protection—
that includes lament, tears, tenderness, and vulnerability.
We know that systems of evil and oppression have cre-
     ated worlds of violence,
where we are scared to show signs of weakness.
Help us, oh God, to remember that in our weaknesses,
     Your strength is made perfect.
And that we deserve to experience the power of our own
     fullness.
Give us wisdom to lay down the costumes we've worn as
     weapons,
so that we may walk (or dance) authentically—
as Your sacred belongings.
Amen and ashé.

A PROMPT FOR MY NEPHEWS

welcome

- What do you need to reconcile about what you've been taught about masculinity to accept that there is a range of masculine expression?

- How has your cultural, familial, or religious upbringing shaped your own views on gender roles?

- When have you expected boys and men to emotionally self-mutilate because of societal expectations of bravery or stoicism?

witness

I have seen how you struggle to find value in loving relationships that do not include sex or self-harm.

And I have watched you run from your emotions like they were serpents out to destroy your "manhood."

I often wonder how comfortable you would become with tenderness if you had more space to explore what a healed version of yourself feels like.

I hope you learn to find closeness within the bond of friends and brotherhood.

I pray I get to witness the fullness of your identity one day.

—love, Auntie.

writual

The call: I _____ (verb or phrase meaning comprehend or accept) that "patriarchy has no gender," and I am _____ (*-ing* word mean to attempt) to dislodge the narrow beliefs assigned to patriarchy from my _____ (word referencing some aspect of your life). I know the truth now, which means I will fight for myself, my nephews, sons, brothers, and friends to have space to _____ (name a truth you want all boys and men to experience).

The response: I/we stand in agreement with who you are becoming. And with God as our witness, we are delighted to welcome your bravery as you strive to exercise spiritual discernment as truth-telling so that others around you are inspired to do the same.

Porch Talk

"Call a Thing a Thing" and Other Lessons from Radical Subjectivity

HONEY, THE PORCH IS CALLING, dusk is falling, the crickets chirping just in time for a few sips (hold the slurping) with your favorite Auntie. I'm serving a variety of tea tonight. Nice, strong and hot—steeped in the deep wells of stories I hadn't told in forever. Whew, chile . . . what a time, what a time! So, let's start with all the Tea first, then we'll get into the honest-to-goodness Truth(s) after that. Here's the tea (as in "oh, that'll *teach*" moments):

- Too growns: Those with sage wisdom and smart mouths get a bad rap for being troublemakers, when really, they're *peacemakers* (see Matthew 5:9).

- Hardheads: Those who typically learn things the hard way might be the very ones who have a hard time believing new truths about themselves—especially if those truths include tenderness.

- Holy rollers: Those struggling with unhealthy theological addiction have a love/hate relationship issue—they love *their version* of the truth more than they hate causing harm to others. #AskMeHowIKnow #RecoveringHolyRoller

- Nephews: Those who are boys and men have likely never been told how much patriarchy inflicts violence and causes them to sedate themselves from feeling love, pain . . . anything.

Now, here's the truth(s), because like good Auntie Iyanla Vanzant has taught us, "Sometimes, you have to call a thing a thing." At some point in my life, Auntie has been a too grown, a hardhead, and a holy roller too. And the thing that folks in these groups, including nephews, have in common is this: many times, they are stuck in patterns of thinking and behavior that avoid accountability and truth-telling. To go a step further, I'd argue that truth and, by extension, truth-telling must be both internalized and expressed with balance, care, and grace within the loving bonds of relationship with God and others. But usually, our perspective of "truth" has been so shaped by systemic oppression hiding in unlikely places (such as faith spaces and familial beliefs) that we end up serving as carriers for the sickness rather than seeking out cures for it. Having been there myself, I know all too well the signs and pitfalls of closed-mindedness that often comes with lack of access to various truths.

When we are socialized to silence ourselves or others because we or they are too grown. Or we shut down our imaginations because we can't see another way to be (or become). Or we proliferate death-dealing and deflating beliefs onto ourselves or others because it's all we know. Or we anesthetize our senses so we can play a part assigned to us all the more easily. When we do these things, we accept a posture of inflexible and uncritical obedience that strips us of the power to discern the complexities and contours of our lives. We are offering ourselves as tributes to hunger games that would eat our souls and demand complicity to the cannibalization of others in our midst. This is the dangerous price we pay when we refuse to consider how we contribute to the suffering of our world. And this is why we must get to the root of what will heal us.

The womanist tenet of radical subjectivity tells us that to rise above our circumstances, we must assume "a defiant posture and audacious, inquisitive nature."[1] It emphasizes the importance of Black women's perspectives and experiences as central to theological reflection and asserts that Black women must be seen as authoritative subjects, capable of defining their own realities and expressing their own spiritual insights. This involves a shift away from traditional theological paradigms that have marginalized or silenced Black women. Personally, I have come to understand radical subjectivity as a means of clawing our way out of the messes we face—whether personal, communal, professional, spiritual—because it places the onus on using my own agency, life experiences, and wisdom to move beyond life's challenges.

How can we expand radical subjectivity to fit or stretch our evolving faith expressions and spirituality in the context of sacred belonging? I offer *truth-telling as spiritual discernment* as a theological commitment because it connects the liberatory nature of womanism (and womanist theology) to the deeply spiritual act of speaking in authority and faith to heal dis-ease around us. Scripture affirms that "death and life are in the power of the tongue" (Proverbs 18:21)—a direct affirmation of our voice as force for good or evil. In this way, truth-telling as spiritual discernment is so full of power and possibility because it turns an otherwise over-spiritualized, sometimes inarticulable, and always individualized faith practice—spiritual discernment—into an act that is wholly concerned with the God-given agency to improve our communities.

What have you been taught about spiritual discernment? I was taught that spiritual discernment was a God-led decision-making process that would give clarity on what to do next. Most of the time, though, it involved some sort of decision about a life transition or relationship that would ultimately benefit me. Rarely, if at all, was spiritual discernment relayed to me as something that should help another person and involved prioritizing another person's well-being above my own. Yet it was preached as a substance of faith that was a fruit of the Spirit and a necessary area for growth for any believer. Therefore, anyone who found themselves in perpetual states of trauma or suffering had to be doing something wrong. As in, they likely lacked a strong sense of spiritual discernment that would miraculously enable them to *see* their way out of poverty or lack or bad relationships or sickness.

This isn't to say that people who are living their best lives have the best discernment—as I've gotten older, I've come to understand there are many more factors to someone's overall success that may not be attributed to their spiritual acumen. My point is only that spiritual discernment was presented to me as a spiritual gifting that enabled someone to be success-ful at walking with God. It was always about an individual alignment with God, rather than actively partnering with God to help someone else.

If you grew up with or have a similar belief about spiritual discernment, the good news is I'm here to sit with you on this here porch and help activate your curiosity about that belief. Because if we stretch our theological imaginations a little bit, we might find there is more to our spirituality than what has been offered to us. Basically, what Auntie is trying to get y'all to do is open up your minds and rethink narrow definitions of spiritual discernment—especially if they are primarily concerned with prosperity-gospel-adjacent theology. Prosperity gospel is a relative of spiritual discernment. It says that if you align with what God wants for your life, you can have nice cars, fancy houses, and so on. It grounds its outcomes in spiritual discernment that focuses on individual success.[2] That kind of "health and wealth" thinking only ever results in more money in your pocket rather than employers offering a living wage in your community so that everyone has more money in their pockets—or in some other version of self-help that couldn't care less about your neighbor. Spiritual discernment can be so much more robust than these flimsy views I was once given. At its weakest potency, sure—spiritual discernment might supply someone with the ability to make sound decisions for their own future. But at its most impactful, spiritual discernment can reveal the most entrenched forms of evil and oppression and actually dare to do something about them.

Let's consider some examples of truth-telling as spiritual discernment and how it disrupts the status quo. Esther (from the biblical accounts), Angela Y. Davis, Sister Mary Clarence (aka Delores Van Cartier as played by Whoopi Goldberg in *Sister Act 1* and *2*), and Meghan Thee Stallion seem like disparate figures. But like too growns, hardheads, holy rollers, and nephews have more in common than we might think, these women share a posture of courageous truth-telling. Esther is recorded as a young Jewish woman in the Persian diaspora who marries the king (thereby becoming queen) and risks her life to foil a wicked plot that would kill her people. Angela Davis is a philosopher and global activist who was targeted by the US government for her radical political views on capitalism and racism and was imprisoned for nearly two years in connection with her service on the Soledad Brothers Defense Committee. Davis was ultimately found not guilty and exonerated of all criminal charges against her. In *Sister Act 1* and *2*, Delores Van Cartier / Sister Mary Clarence is a Las Vegas showgirl turned Witness Protection Program participant whose cover is as a nun in a convent. In both movies, Sister Mary Clarence becomes a voice in the wilderness despite being asked to play a subservient and meek role to aid others around her. Lastly, there is Meghan Thee Stallion—hip-hop and rap music sensation who received severe backlash after speaking up about a shooting she endured at the hands of another (male) rapper.

All these women (whether factual or fictive) moved from being passive subjects to active speakers on behalf of themselves and others who might experience harm. It was not enough that they noticed systems of suppression and fear-based compliance. It was not enough for them to simply obey their way into self-safety. It was not enough for them to shut their eyes to the realities of danger that awaited them and their communities. They were, instead, willful agents working in authority and collaboration with divine help to call attention to their plight and stop forthcoming suffering. Their capacity to see and speak truth to power became a light shining the way toward a better future and uncovering the darknesses lurking in their midst. And their very willingness to commit to such truth-telling enabled others to know the truth, understand what they may have never before comprehended or seen, and make different choices. Auntie translation: truth-telling as spiritual discernment *always* helps folks learn to walk and chew gum at the same time. I don't use this idiom flippantly or pejoratively. Truth-telling as spiritual discernment gives us wisdom to move forward (walk) toward solutions while we figure out how to break down what keeps us stuck (chew gum) and spit it out in the form of necessary truth.

Have you ever swallowed gum before? Do you know what happens to it? The body can't digest it or gain any nutrients from it. So eventually the indigestible object is removed from your body as waste. What a shame it would be if we allowed our most pressing truths to be swallowed and extricated as waste rather than speaking them in ways that result in well-being, wholeness, and wisdom for others and ourselves. So, let me say this to you loud and clear—your body isn't meant to digest that which is otherwise unpalatable and indigestible. You are not meant to swallow your tongue in fear of how your voice might upset the masses of people who may have already drank the Kool-Aid of oppression. You will gain no points or nutrients from sitting in full-mouthed silence. However, the freedom and liberation of others is bound up in your ability to overcome whatever barriers hinder you from exercising your God-given right to speak truth boldly and intentionally.

I hope this is tracking with you so far and we are beginning to unravel some of the pesky beliefs or misnomers that limit our experiences with sacred belonging. Because truth-telling as spiritual discernment is a simple yet profound way to take the first steps toward aligning our private wrestling with our public witness. It is a way to allow our color-fullnesses to spill over onto the forcibly whitewashed canvases that line the hallways of our thoughts and actions. It is the way to start seeing ourselves as co-conspirators with a God who is on the side of the oppressed.[3] It is our way into cultivating sacred belonging for ourselves, our loved ones, and people with whom we may otherwise never connect. Think about the power of the recent #MeToo movement, where thousands of women began bravely telling their stories of sexual abuse and trauma. This powerful narrative of truth-telling revolutionized how we talk about harm and hold perpetrators of sexual violence accountable for their actions.

But how do we get started, Reverend Auntie, when truth-telling as a form of spiritual discernment is perhaps new and likely uncomfortable for us? I figured y'all might be struggling with that, but don't worry. It's been difficult for me to do at times, and I understand it can be uncomfortable at first. But I got you covered with a few tips that should help you get started.

Tip 1: Truth-telling starts with attuning your ears and heart to the layers of truth that have gone unnoticed. You can learn these truths by cultivating intentional relationships with people who are different from you. However, let Auntie hasten to give you a word of caution. Do not begin probing people you barely know about their darkest, deepest secrets. That is absolutely not the move.

Instead, you can expand and explore your worldview by reading nonfiction (including memoirs), poetry, and other storytelling written for and by people who have various intersecting identities that are outside of your comfort zone. Were you, like me, raised to believe that it was better for same-gender-loving people not to act on those attractions? (Sheesh,

I cringed just typing that.) Then perhaps you should prioritize reading works by LGBTQIA+ authors and creators. Have you struggled to understand the layered, sometimes interwoven, issues that affect women? Maybe you can start by researching movies, plays, and documentaries that elevate the complexities of womanhood from modern to contemporary times. Then (and only then) might you consider exploring more in-depth conversations with trusted loved ones and friends about what you are learning and any lived experiences they want to share with you.

If you are not in close relationships with people from different backgrounds, then Google, social media groups, and content creators are your friends. Let the algorithm coders work in your favor and curate your social media feeds with voices amplifying messages that you'd like to learn more about. The key is to be intentional in seeking out truth so that you are a more inclusive, nuanced, and thoughtful truth-teller.

Tip 2: Be proactive in defining spiritual discernment as part and parcel of disrupting systemic patterns of oppression. I ain't gonna lie. This one will be tricky sometimes because each of us comes programmed with our own set of privileges or other barriers that impede us from being empathetic to the ways our laws, policies, and practices are built on white supremacy and other forms of evil. Yet by connecting our capacity to engage in spiritual discernment with a willingness to call out systems of unfairness, we turn those weapons on their heads and point out the rightful villains.

It is the difference between saying to a loved one, "I know you've been struggling financially—here's $20 I can loan you," versus saying, "Our economic system is failing all of us because capitalism functions best when there are haves and have nots;

therefore, I am going to not only support you in finding a living wage and advocating for higher pay where I can, but I will also babysit your kids so that you can find rest from your weariness." Can you hear the difference in that? One statement provides no indictment of a system that prides itself on pillaging our productivity while paying us pennies and instead offers charity as a one-time event. The other lays blame where it is due and offers ongoing support with tangible service and truth-telling to advocate on others' behalf.

Tip 3: Practice truth-telling through writing, whispering, then proclaiming it in front of witnesses. Sometimes it can be hard to tell the truth even when it's necessary. That's why I'm offering you three steps to help you cultivate that discipline.

First, writing about it helps get the issue out of your head and on to a screen or paper. If you haven't done the writuals at the end of each chapter, they can be a way to jump-start the process. (You might want to do them again with this intention more clearly in mind.) Second, begin reciting things that you are passionate about in front of a mirror at home or while you're in the bathroom alone. I like to whisper them to myself as reminders that sync into my body. If this seems strange to you, it's okay. The point is to begin speaking the truth softly so that one day you can say it loudly. The last part of this process is to say what you need to say within contexts where you feel comfortable and accountable. Are there generational traumas hovering within your family dynamics that you are serious about disrupting? Begin speaking up in family settings more often and asking a loved one to be a support as you do. Has something happened at your job that affected you or a colleague? Consult an HR professional about the issue and create a plan to address the problem.

Tip 4: Truth-telling as spiritual discernment will require you to develop healthy coping mechanisms in the face of potential adversity and backlash. Listen to Auntie, dear ones. Truth-telling is not for the faint of heart or the weak. And when you begin practicing this discipline more consistently, publicly, and vocally, you will open yourself up to trolling, pushback, and sometimes more dire consequences. This is why I encourage you to have a system of support (including but not limited to a therapist, a close circle of friends or advisors, and a strong prayer/meditation life) because you will need it in order to maintain your wholeness and clarity of mind. Be kind and tender with yourself. Truth-telling requires an inward (and outward) vulnerability. And be wise enough to protect yourself with good cybersecurity measures, check-in protocols with friends, and whatever else will help you rest free from worry.

I know this is a lot to comprehend and consider. So, I want to ask: How you are processing these things, and how's your heart? It can be hard and scary to learn a new thing and embrace parts of ourselves that we've been insecure about or never realized lay hidden within us. But that's the best part of learning truth-telling as spiritual discernment. You begin to experience your own magnitude and depth in a fresh new way—and that, my friend, is what I call a sacred belonging. A manifestation of your highest and most authentic self.

I shared earlier about third-grade me who was bullied by my teacher and how my mother leavened me unto life. Time eventually gave me the words for truth-telling, which turned into a poem that I want to share here to show you what truth-telling can feel, look, and sound like.

it was third grade
when i finally discovered
the lyrics of my favorite song
were an incantation
to ward off evil
pale-faced women.

sitting in the back
of momma's '92 honda accord
we'd ride with the windows down
whisking from grocery store to church
singing our secular tune
that carried sacred wisdom—
gospel to my prepubescent hearing—
which was weighed down
by poisonous words
hanging on me like earrings
from the teacher
who'd never had
a Black girl
like me.

"I can cast a spell of secrets you can tell
Mix a special brew, put fire inside of you
. . . I'm every woman"[4]

danger and fear
were the twin demons
that had replaced
the grace and mercy
pastor always preached about

and they followed me
into the schoolhouse
everyday—
scolding me
with scalding hot words
that burned a fire inside of me.
"you'll never be able to spell
at the rate you're going—"
she embarrassed me
in front of class one day.
and the flames grew
and grew in me
the burning desire
to cast a spell
she would never
recover from.

so, naturally
i signed myself up
for the school talent show
where i lip-synced
the incantation
that Whitney and Chaka
gave me words to
and waited patiently
for something magical
to happen.

only my pale-faced teacher
was surprised when it did.
because that bit of spellwork

conjured up the warrior
living inside my momma
when she appeared outta thin air
up at my school
to get the teacher and principal
on the same page
of understandin'
and get me outta class for the day—
assuring me that Mrs. Pale-face
would never mess with me again.

from that day forward,
i knew.
that every woman
i ever needed
was inside of me
and momma and Whitney too. [5]

From the early nineties school talent show to now, I have learned to harness the fierceness of Whitney Houston, the courageousness of my momma, and the brilliance of countless other Black women who have helped mold and shape me. While it hasn't always been easy, it's been both necessary and worth it. And I believe that it will be worth it for you, too. So take this as your Auntie gently (but not so gently) nudging you to give truth-telling a chance. There's really no telling how many lives you may save—even your own—by doing so.

Tribe Is Sanctuary

Now a man from the house of Levi went and married a Levite woman. The woman conceived and bore a son, and when she saw that he was a fine baby, she hid him three months. When she could hide him no longer she got a papyrus basket for him and plastered it with bitumen and pitch; she put the child in it and placed it among the reeds on the bank of the river. His sister stood at a distance, to see what would happen to him.

—Exodus 2:1–4

We all we got.

—Black American translation of "ubuntu," African proverb meaning "I am because we are."

FIVE

To My Babies and Fools

(People Who Don't Know No Better)

A PARABLE FOR MY BABIES AND FOOLS

"The Lord watches over babies and fools" is a well-known saying in Black culture. Adapted from a passage in Psalm 116, the phrase speaks to the belief that God accompanies and covers those who simply cannot look out for themselves. In some extra-special cases, though, the saying is shortened to just "babies and fools," often when trying to be less harsh in speaking on a person who has gotten into yet another unnecessary and completely avoidable situation. And I certainly must hurry to say that I thank God for divine protection when I was both a baby and a fool.

I remember one summer during my early teenage years when family was in town visiting us in Arkansas. I just so happened to have a fresh new perm, so my hair was bone straight with a crisp bump of curl at the end. My birthday had just passed, so I likely had donned a brand-new outfit and clean pair of shoes. And with the freshly laid doo and styling digs, I just knew I was finer than fine.

I remember walking around our small home, packed full of my cousins, talking about how good I looked. In between my applying more lip gloss and strutting my stuff, my mom's cousin (whom I think of as an Auntie because of her age) finally stopped me and asked me if I thought I looked good. To which I swiftly answered yes. My cousin/auntie nicely and directly responded something to the effect of, Well, if you know you look so good, why do you have to keep telling us about it? Her question stumped me. And after a few moments of not being able to come up with a smart retort, I quietly sat down and promptly began minding my own business— which instantly shifted the atmosphere and made space for everyone to enjoy one another's company far more than when I'd been boasting about my outward appearance.

You see, what I was guilty of back then was "smelling myself," as the Black elders like to say. And when you're smelling yourself, you are quite the example of self-absorption, and essentially no one can tell you anything. However, let us not confuse smelling yourself with being hardheaded. As we talked about earlier, hardheads are those who are strong-willed and usually learn things the hard way. Those smelling themselves are just in a temporary phase of overindulgence in their self-identified best qualities—which makes them extremely susceptible to folly. From about the age of fifteen to sixteen, I found myself slipping and sliding into this unfortunate phase. And every single time, someone from my family or my village got me right together. Saving me from myself and any more needless mistakes.

I think these "let me help you out" moments are a beautiful illustration of what sanctuary and safety actually look like. And given how our current sociopolitical reality is rife with conflict, public health concerns, and global wars, it seems appropriate to consider what sanctuary really means. For those of us raised in the Western context of the United States, we are homegrown, raised, and reared in the crops of rugged individualism. How do I know this? Think about one of the most pervasive narratives we are taught from birth about America: the American Dream. Which tells us that anyone (allegedly) with the will and determination enough to pull themselves up by their bootstraps can go from underdog to uber successful. Undergirding this "hard work pays off" narrative is the idea that you, by your own merits, can lift yourself from your circumstances and overcome whatever barriers to get to your goal. Sure, that sounds nice. But rarely, if ever, is that how success works. For those on the margins, most who have found some modicum of wealth driven by a sense of purpose have been supported widely and deeply by networks of church members, family, friends, and neighbors. Even people with the most privilege and wealth are typically *not* self-made. They, too, have had loads of help in the form of trust funds, legacy admissions into Ivy League schools, and other family or network advantages that most people do not have.

I find it quite sad (and comical) that we allow our social narrative of the American Dream to reinforce this false belief about individual fortitude. But I digress. My larger point is that when we find ourselves facing threats of danger or uncertainty, our subconscious beliefs about our own efficacy and ability to "succeed" also shape how we try to secure our safety. Well, if you ask me, this is an absolutely foolish way to govern ourselves and our thoughts. We seem to collectively conduct ourselves within American politics, ethics, and identity the same way I was smelling myself when I was fifteen. We sometimes have an "America first, America forever" mentality that really stinks up the place. And just like my cousin/auntie had to come gather me, I am about to help gather us.

When we change our perceptions of what sanctuary is and its function in our lives, I believe we will also better respond to conflicts locally and globally. This is because, for those of us serious about pursuing sacred belonging, we understand that sanctuary is not simply a place bound by architecture or region or nationality; rather, it is an intentional effort and way of being with one another—so that we all may experience safety together. We can't just be so full of ourselves as to think that our safety will ever be achieved in isolation. Rather, a *sanctuary* mindset becomes a real-time foil for white supremacist ideals cloaked in widely accepted narratives like the American Dream.

I've touched on white supremacy in earlier chapters, but we might as well lay it out here. White supremacy is an interlocking set of beliefs, practices, and laws that work together to maintain power for a "ruling" class and relegate marginalized persons (such as Black, Indigenous, Latinx, LGBTQIA+, people with disabilities, migrants) to subordinate roles, jobs, and other functions that result in lived consequences. White supremacy relies on the idea that white people and the ideas, thoughts, beliefs, and actions of white people are superior to those of Black people, Indigenous people, and other people of color. Because white supremacy relies on people to play their parts—whether knowingly or unknowingly—it is nourished when we fall into the trap of individualism, which says that "I" matter over and above any and everyone else. When we are less prone to care about our neighbors, we are more prone to carry the water of white supremacy—watering its seeds, thus assisting its growth.

So if prioritizing your individual self strengthens white supremacy, then it seems right that focusing on the collective good of others may be the answer to weakening it. When we support one another—especially across lines of difference—we chip away at the power of white supremacy. And I believe that engaging in the work of building sanctuary with and among one another helps us do that. Now, let Auntie tell you what that means practically speaking. All that self-segregation y'all (by y'all, I mean all of us) like to do—whether in your cute little churches or on your little neighborhood blocks—is not gonna work. Most of us build our circles of safety and community in comfort zones that are by and large homogeneous. Even if our "home bases" aren't homogeneous, we seldom open the door for someone who thinks differently, lives differently, or looks different to take up space and offer alternative perspectives. So just as I was doing the most and "smelling myself" with my cousins—thereby taking up all the space for myself—I fear we are far too comfortable existing in these self-blown bubbles that make no room for Others.

During my first semester of field education placement at seminary, I was placed at a historically Black church that was navigating their way through becoming a welcoming and affirming church for LGBTQIA+ people. For context, the denomination had voted to become welcoming, but it wanted individual churches to go at their own pace since it would require quite a theological shift in policy and church practice. At that church, I met two openly gay Black women who planned to marry one another. During one Bible study, when the church was deep in the throes of that wrestling, I used Romans 8:35–39 to justify that whole "love the sinner, hate the sin" idea. And Whitney, who is now one of my very dearest friends, snapped back and said it was that kind of attitude that caused her sincere harm and pushed her further away from God and the church.

Like the moment with my cousin/auntie, rather than respond, I decided to sit there in the discomfort and just listen. What she'd said is that she was hindered in experiencing the fragrance and presence of an all-loving God because what I just said was funky and foul enough to turn her away. In the weeks and months after that incident, I learned how to hold space instead of taking up too much space with my narrow views. I came to know these two women—Whitney and Rasheeda—as more than just folks I saw in the pews from Sunday to Sunday. I began to regard them as friends, neighbors, and sisters. That meant that what concerned them, concerned me. When they experienced more harm at our church and decided to take a break from attending for a while, they invited me into their home to sit in their pain with them. When they had married and became pregnant with their first child, they invited me to be their first babysitter. And when we both lost parents unexpectedly, we hugged one another long and hard. They became my tribe, a chosen family, and I became theirs. And together, regardless of our differences, we learned how to do life and build sanctuary *together*.

What I gained from being in genuine relationship with Whitney and Rasheeda was priceless. Their unwavering love and unapologetic identities grew me from being an educated fool to an empathetic friend. No longer was I okay with Bible-thumping people to death with scripture. Instead, I began leavening and loving people to life as Jesus commanded us to do. You know, the kinda important ones like "Love your neighbor as yourself" and "Do to others as you would have them do to you"? For me, that's the whole entire point of being Jesus followers and decent humans.

But sometimes, like babies and fools, we don't know what we don't know. And until someone comes and changes us—whether by changing our smelly diapers or helping us change our odorous ways—we suffer in ignorance and cause harm in our wake. I thank God for the folks in my tribe who have changed me. Both when I was a baby and a fool. Because without them, I would've stayed where I was and never would've become who God intended me to be. I guess it's true what they say. The Lord truly does watch over babies and fools.

A PRAYER FOR MY BABIES AND FOOLS

God who covers us,
we thank You for not faulting us for our faults,
nor leaving us stuck in our smelly places.
And we ask forgiveness for all the times that our foolish-
    ness kept us from seeing the way to be better versions
    of ourselves.
God, help us to accept love, support, and wisdom from
    others who are unlike us
so that we may learn how to be Your sanctuary—where
    everyone might find rest and refuge.
May we endeavor to build safe spaces among one another
    as our effort to create sacred belonging.
Amen and ashé.

A PROMPT FOR MY BABIES AND FOOLS

welcome

- Do you have any memories of being so foolish that you thought you knew everything? How did that attitude permeate your way of being with others?

- How have American or Western idealism and other social narratives shaped the way you view systems of support or sanctuary?

- What might be difficult to navigate when attempting to build sanctuary with people who have different beliefs from you?

witness

I have seen you get stuck in patterns of isolation.
Because you think your livelihood depends solely on you.
And I have seen how you've struggled to maintain a
    sense of safety,
when the world seems to be drowning in chaos and fear.
Yet you deserve to feel the pleasantness of inclusion—
one that envelops your senses in the warm embrace of
    radical acceptance and mutual accountability.
I hope I get to see you in that sanctuary one day.

                                   —love, Auntie.

writual

The call: I understand that it is _____ (word meaning okay or acceptable) to not know what I don't know. And that it is God's grace that will allow me to _____ (phrase that refers to being in relationship with new and different people) so that I might learn that which my eyes have never seen. I am grateful for the opportunity to _____ (phrase meaning to create community) as a soft and safe place for my neighbors and my community.

The response: I/we stand in agreement with the great cloud of witnesses whose love is diverse and divine. I/we support people in their fullness because I/we refuse to let anyone bear false witness against their own humanity. I/we receive the abundant love enfolded in the sanctuary of beloved community.

SIX

To My Beloveds

(People Who Show Us a Better Way to Do Faith and Community)

A PARABLE FOR MY BELOVEDS

When I was in my early twenties, I missed out on the party of the century. It wasn't just any old, run-of-the-mill college frat party, either. No, it was *the* livest event of the year. Everybody who was anybody was going. And, well, Auntie must have been a self-imposed nobody—because I decided not to join in on the fun. You see, the time had come for the university's annual drag show as hosted by an alliance of student groups on campus. Every year, the show had a unique theme and huge participation from student performers. It drew record crowds, from entertainment-seeking students to party-going fanatics.

I was not among them. I know, I know. Your FOMO (fear of missing out) is likely yelling, "But why, Auntie?" My answer is both basic (in the worst way) and ludicrous: I was "too saved/holy" to allow myself to go. Coming from where I'm from—a small, Bible-belted town in the American South—I'd never known anyone who was outwardly gay or transgender. So, when I went off to college, I found myself in a sea of people who had way different experiences and backgrounds. And I was struggling to stay afloat. I remember one of my classmates in particular, whom I'll call Savion. He was amazing and fun and so brilliant in every way. I enjoyed seeing him on campus or in the cafe. He was literally the funniest person I'd ever met. But when he made plans to perform at the annual drag show, I drew the line.

Savion was an out, gay, Black man. Likely the first I'd ever met. And I'm ashamed to admit that I made so many mistakes around him—misgenderings and horrible assumptions escaped from my mouth before I had the language and awareness to know how to be a better human and ally to people beyond my black-and-white definitions of masculine and feminine.

All our friends were excited for Savion, of course. Many of the young women in our friend group helped find the dress Savion would perform in, picked out the best makeup and wig to complement his skin, and even gave pointers on his routine. Where they became loud supporters ready to show up, I became a silent critic on the sideline.

I could not associate myself with something as ungodly as a drag show. Or so I thought.

Years of biblical teaching on immorality, abomination, and being "yoked together with unbelievers" had made it so difficult for me to see the beauty of what was right in front of me. I vividly recall the night of the performance. Right around the time the drag show let out, I happened to be going for a midnight breakfast snack (customary college student behavior). I saw people of all different races, backgrounds, genders, and nationalities dancing and laughing and hugging and high-fiving. All my friends were surrounding Savion and congratulating him on what must've been an amazing performance. Too bad I wouldn't know it from seeing it with my own eyes.

As they gushed about how much fun they'd had, Savion absolutely beamed. Radiated light and positive energy. Something I rarely saw happen in the four walls of any church I'd attended. It was like a legitimate Pentecost of pantyhose, press-on nails, and those precious in God's sight, all in one. It was people from every nation and tongue speaking the same language of love and celebration. It was the beloved community I'd pray about at night but miss out on by day—simply because it did not come packaged the way I wanted, or expected, it to look. I didn't attend, because I chose to miss out on the occasion. And I missed out on the abundance found in a community of folks who cared for and loved themselves and others deeply.

The reality is that I was scared (read: homophobic). So I chose perceived safety over my own discomfort because it was more convenient than showing up for someone I considered a friend. What's even more unfortunate is that I did this in the name of a "holiness" that seemed to conveniently forget how Jesus invited everyone to His table. Here is where I wish I had the ability to time-travel in real life rather than through my writing. Because if I'd been able to fast-forward from my undergraduate days to my seminary days, I would have been so much more clear about the power of real sanctuary.

In my last letter, I wrote about how I served at a church that was wrestling with whether to become a welcoming and affirming space for LGBTQIA+ people. During that time, I took a leap of faith and watched a documentary entitled *For the Bible Tells Me So*. The movie follows several families as they grapple with religious beliefs, structural discrimination, and toxic theologies after their loved ones come out as gay. Several pastors, religious scholars, and everyday church people discuss how scripture has been interpreted to support the condemnation of LGBTQIA+ people while also explaining the fuller context of these scriptures and offering alternative ways to approach those texts.

That movie helped me to take my faith a step further after the pivot I made when I attempted to tell my former pastor about my calling to ministry. As I've described, he, too, was adept at a brand of literal interpretation of Scripture that absolutely meant that I—along with all other women—should remain silent in the church. And just as that disruptive event taught me to allow room for reading the Bible with an awareness of the historical context concerning women, I also had to be deliberate in rereading scriptures that I believed had clearly spelled out homosexuality as sin. And while I won't try to unpack every scripture concerning homosexuality here, suffice it to say I now believe that same-gender-loving people are made in God's image and that their love is an outpouring of God's love. This is unequivocally *not* the same issue that Paul describes in the New Testament concerning sexual immorality and unnatural relations, which many scholars believe are directed to address improper abuse of enslaved humans and nonconsensual relationships with young boys or children. Additionally, Old Testament scriptures referring to same-gender relations as an abomination actually speak to the wasting of seed (as in semen) as the offense given the divine laws concerning preserving Israel's people in perpetuity.[1]

Given this new way of approaching the Bible, I was able to learn how to be a better friend to persons I would have formerly cast aside in rigid judgment. And it gave me much needed room to stretch my hands toward figuring out what connects us to one another rather than sitting up in my room (in the famous words of Brandy) by myself when I could've been having the time of my life while supporting someone who was simply trying to express their fullness. Savion knew the truth well before I did. He knew how to exercise grace and joy and love. He knew how to dress up and sing and dance and be his beautiful self—creating sanctuary for others to experience so that they could also have permission to walk in their own truth.

To this day, I hate that I opted out of such a transformative and life-giving experience. But I hope you will opt in, beloved.

Dominator culture has tried to keep us all afraid, to make us choose safety instead of risk, sameness instead of diversity. Moving through that fear, finding out what connects us, reveling in our differences; this is the process that brings us closer, that gives us a world of shared values, of meaningful community.[2]
—bell hooks, *Teaching Community*

A PRAYER FOR MY BELOVEDS
God who shows up where two or three are gathered,
we praise You for allowing us to see your magnitude
with, and among, the marginalized.

Thank You for the unfolding of love and splendor
that is found in the unlikeliest of places
and in the embrace of the most unique people.
Help us, oh God, to understand our salvation
as bound up in the freedom and liberation
of our multigender neighbors and colorful kin.
Rather than in conforming to the blandness
of a whitewashed world,
free us from the beliefs that keep us bound to rules
and create harmful boundaries around God's daily bread.
But give us wisdom, instead, to create beloved
    community
when and wherever we enter.
Remove from us any fear that has been instilled in us
to hide our fullnesses and expect the same from Others.
Now, may the God of all and every gender
continue to mold us into vessels
to pour out God's lavish love
upon all creation
so that every person becomes
a receptacle for abundant care and sacred belonging.
Amen and ashé.

A PROMPT FOR MY BELOVEDS
welcome

- Do you have formative (i.e., substantive, close, spacious)
  relationships with people of varying gender identities,
  other races, or religious or cultural backgrounds? If so,
  describe those relationships. If not, think aspiration-
  ally about what that might look like to pursue those
  relationships.

- How has fear of the Other or the unknown affected your ability to show up and enjoy new experiences?

- When have you felt the need to hide parts of yourself to keep peace with your family or other people in places you frequent?

- What might be at stake (socially, spiritually, culturally, politically) when you prioritize harmful boundaries over, and against, beloved community?

witness

I have seen you pinch yourself into numbness.

Hold your breath to account for the weight of everyone else's expectations.

Go along with the crowd to get along with what they said was acceptable.

But you will not find refuge in the status quo.

Nor discover a safe space to be seen when you hide so well.

Give yourself permission to breathe.

I pray you feel what it is like to be held by an embrace that frees you when everyone else said it was forbidden.

You deserve love in abundance and multitudes.

—love, Auntie.

writual

The call: I will know the _____ (noun that describes a characteristic you enjoy) of relationships with people I have not _____ (phrase that explains what has stopped you from knowing others). I admit that my lack of relationship with _____ (describe a group or persons who are different from you that you desire to know) was aided and abetted by external pressures of _____ (name a relevant harmful belief or practice). I will no longer allow such pressure to stop me from being free to enjoy _____ (phrase that builds upon your first fill in the blank).

The response: I/we stand in agreement with the great cloud of witnesses whose love is diverse and divine. I/we support people in their fullness because I/we refuse to let anyone bear false witness against their own humanity. I/we receive the abundant love enfolded in the sanctuary of beloved community.

SEVEN

To My Blessed Hearts

(People Who Have Been Harmed or Just Do Stupid Stuff)

A PARABLE FOR MY BLESSED HEARTS

When I think of sanctuary, I think of Black women. Not the kind of sanctuary of safety or salvation only concerned with my soul. But the kind of safety that has everything to do with the flesh. You see, when I have been closest to the brink of destruction, it was Black women whose liberating words and presence set me free of my most dangerous self-deprecation, invited me to love myself tenderly, and challenged me to own myself as a sacred belonging in a world that said I belonged to everyone else but myself.

I think of Mrs. Morrow, who was a staple at the financial office at Vanderbilt University. How she greeted me and my concerned parents with the information that we needed to know that I could financially *and* academically survive at a

PWI (predominantly white institution) hundreds of miles away from home. I think of the myriad aunties I enjoyed growing up—both by blood and by bond—the ones who watched me when Momma was working, who gave hand-me-downs when Momma couldn't make ends meet, who prepared a most holy table of bread and Kool-Aid before I was even allowed to take communion in the pews.

I think of my mother and my grandmas and my big mama who knew the Lord but also laid down the law, each in their own ways. These women who birthed me, whupped me when I needed it, wiped tears, whipped up magic before #BlackGirlMagic was a thing, and *made miracles every Thanksgiving* (shout-out, Tupac). And I think of the young women I met in my freshman dorm who would become my big sisters and line sisters of my sorority, who introduced me to who I would become and valued the nerdy Black girl who had never found her place in high school.

You see, my fellow blessed hearts, when I was a freshman in college, I was simultaneously super smart and really dumb at the same time. I had an uncanny ability to put my foot in my mouth at the absolute worst moments. Take, for example, the time I was at church with my mom (likely a couple of years before I went off to college) and I told a lady that she looked "really nice with her makeup on." Sounds harmless— but sis clearly took quick offense. I've never seen my momma snatch me up by the arm so fast. And even more unfortunate for me, it was the first of many "oh no, baby, what are you doing" moments.

By the time I matriculated into Vanderbilt as an undergraduate, I continued to say the most awkward and unbecoming things. One day I was doing some community service along with many of my peers and new friends. We were volunteering with the Deltas (members of Delta Sigma Theta Sorority, Inc.), as was the custom for young women who wanted to join the organization. We were mentoring and tutoring at a local HBCU, and the members of the sorority were asking us various questions to break the ice with the high schoolers in attendance. I have no idea what the question was or why I would have thought this was remotely appropriate to say, but I answered, "Yeah, we all have to learn to deal with cocky Caucasians." Yikes bikes! Now, the funny thing is, that statement is very on brand for nearly forty-year-old Auntie to say. But back then I was not yet that pointed of a truth-teller. To my complete horror, the members of the sorority looked so taken aback by my response that one of them so graciously cleaned it up on my behalf while I silently cringed from the embarrassment.

There were a couple more occasions where I said the absolute darndest (read: dumbest) things in the presence of the Deltas, all of whom would be deciding my fate to join the sorority the next year. Thank God for me (and my chance to make it into the chapter), one of the members pulled me to the side and reassured me that I'd be fine. I was a solid candidate and a value-add to the organization. Yet even in her graciousness, that member still got me right together and told me, under no uncertain terms, to think way harder and much longer before I spoke. Because if I didn't, she wouldn't be able to save me from myself many more times.

Her one-time benevolence was all I needed. That singular "Bless your heart but don't embarrass me again" was both a warning and prayer. A warning that careless chatter can cause harm, and a prayer that despite careless moments, someone (or something, i.e., grace) was there to cover me, watch out for me, and help me make it to my destination safely—a sanctuary I needed but didn't even know it at the time. In my case, my destination was becoming an esteemed member of Delta Sigma Theta Sorority, Inc.—a space where I would find my chosen family and understand the beauty of sanctuary as found in genuine sisterhood.

As a child, one of the first biblical examples I learned of sisterhood was that of Miriam at the edge of the Nile, watching over her baby brother. According to the book of Exodus, the Egyptian pharaoh had ordered all male children be drowned in the Nile River because he was riddled with fear-based, oppressive leadership syndrome. Yet when Moses was born, an unlikely tribe of women—his mother, his sister Miriam, and the pharaoh's daughter who would become his caretaker—created a cocoon of care around Moses and, ultimately, saved his life despite Pharaoh's genocidal edict.

Most people focus immediately on the fact that Pharaoh's daughter acted graciously, allowing a Jewish maidservant (who also happened to be Moses's birth mother) to nurse the newborn until he was old enough to be taken into her home and raised as her own son. However, I want to focus on young Miriam—Moses's biological sister who waited on the shores of the Nile River to watch over her baby brother and make sure he made it to a place of sanctuary. Not only did Miriam wait to see what would happen to her brother, but she was also cunning and wise enough to suggest finding a Hebrew woman to breastfeed the newborn baby. Upon agreement by Pharaoh's daughter, Miriam brought her mother to nurse and look after Moses (whose original name we do not know) until he was weaned.

Even in the midst of great stress and, likely, the heavy grief over the reality that her beloved brother would not be able to grow up in their home, Miriam still had the sense of mind to create a network of connection for Moses. This connection would be a source of care and preserve Moses's cultural identity—which would become vitally important when he later assumed his God-given role to liberate his people from slavery. Perhaps this is one of the most salient and significant hallmarks of understanding *tribe as sanctuary*: even in the midst of real peril, divinely positioned people will keep you covered from harm *while* keeping you connected to your true identity. There is no higher or better place of refuge than this form of sanctuary.

This sanctuary cannot be bound to physical location or tied to restrictive dogma or doctrine. Instead, tribe as sanctuary is a dynamic space of collaboration wherein the members create rules of engagement and healthy boundaries around that which is deemed sacred. And despite the emergent evangelical trend of denouncing Greek affiliations (i.e., sororities and fraternities), I contend that I first began to experience and embody tribe as sanctuary within my sorority bond of sisterhood. My would-be Big Sister stepped up and advocated for me just like Moses's big sister, intent on keeping watch over me rather than letting me go adrift downriver.

Years after I'd joined the sorority, she (along with other Big Sisters) would keep me tethered to who I had always been and who I would become. Rather than continue to let me make mistakes or, when I was chapter president, lead with inexperience and naivete, they would nurse me back to health, provide wisdom and nourishment, and then send me on my way—time after time. I know, I know. Everyone doesn't have the opportunity or privilege to join such an organization in their lifetime. And that's okay. Because *anyone* can create a tribe as sanctuary experience for themselves with the right heart and mindset.

Tribe as sanctuary means those in your chosen sphere of care never do life alone, nor do they face obstacles without systems of support. Tribe as sanctuary means shouting loudly for the celebrations and standing firmly (but gently) in tender times when accountability is needed most. Tribe as sanctuary reconciles that even Jesus chose an unlikely crew of misfits as He began His ministry—because He understood that purpose didn't need perfection to be successful, it needs people who will see you and stand with you. Lastly, tribe as sanctuary is both lovingly protective of its members and intentional in practicing intersectionality.* Intersectionality, a term coined by scholar Kimberlé Crenshaw, helps us understand how different aspects of a person's identity, such as race, gender, class, sexuality, and more, can merge and overlap and, depending on the context, result in unique experiences of discrimination or privilege. Intersectionality is important because I want to be clear that tribe as sanctuary does not mean tribalism or an "us versus them" ideology. Many of us in the Western world remain preoccupied with that line of thinking. Tribe as sanctuary, rather, insists on seeing how other people's and other groups' struggles for liberation, joy, and safety are bound up and intrinsically linked with our own struggle for the same.

Just as two apparent opposites—Miriam (a Jew) and Pharaoh's daughter (an Egyptian)—represent archetypal enemies who came together to offer sanctuary for Moses to have a thriving life, tribe as sanctuary *must also* be concerned with overturning ideological differences to replace them with opportunities for care. Aboriginal elder and activist Lilla Watson and others put it this way: "If you have come to help me, you are wasting your time. If you have come because your liberation is bound up with mine, then let us work together."[1] Put even more simply, civil rights legend and honorary auntie Fannie Lou Hamer said, "Nobody's free until everybody's free."[2]

Maybe this sounds silly, but if more people gave themselves over to the theological commitment of tribe as sanctuary, there might be fewer blessed hearts in the world. Not because people causing harm or saying dumb stuff would miraculously cease. But simply because, despite those harms, an intentional web of people would be there as a soft place to land and a necessary system of accountability and truth.

Think of all the people who have mass-exited the church at large or forsaken traditional religious spaces. Many of them shudder when church or religious beliefs are mentioned because they have been repeatedly hurt by these same institutions. Yet I figure that if these very people were scooped out of the river of despair, if the truth was told about the oppressive beliefs that got them there, and if they were met with folks prepared to nurse them and encourage their growth, droves of them would be able to heal their stories of church-hurt and trauma. And perhaps one day, like Moses, they might become the ones who deliver us from our internalized and externalized oppressions. Because as Auntie likes to say, like others before her, we are truly all we got.

A PRAYER FOR MY BLESSED HEARTS

God who keeps us,
we thank You for scooping us into Your arms,

when we were either unwanted or endangered.
We ask that You would send Miriams into our midst—
who will watch over us when we cannot.
God, give us tribes of love and care straight from Your
heart to our homes
so that we are truly living sanctuaries—embodied safe
spaces for all
and Your sacred belonging.
Amen and ashé.

A PROMPT FOR MY BLESSED HEARTS

welcome

- How do you respond when people are harmed in your presence or by someone's actions?

- Where have you experienced the safety and freedom found in spaces of sanctuary? Describe what that feels like.

- Have you experienced sanctuary in any faith spaces? Why or why not?

witness

I have seen you going adrift on rivers of danger and
uncertainty.
And I have watched over you because I care about what
happens to you.
I hope you will meet others along your journey who will
not rest until they see about you.
To make sure you are well fed, well loved, and well seen.
You deserve the tribe of your dreams—so that all of who
you are is safe.

—love, Auntie.

writual

The call: I understand that I am both _____ (positive attribute) and _____ (word meaning flawed). And that, even with these traits, I deserve to have a _____ (a phrase that is a synonym for tribe or sanctuary) where I am free to be all of me and blessed to be held within the grace of accountability and truth.

The response: I/we stand in agreement with the great cloud of witnesses whose love is diverse and divine. I/we support people in their fullness because I/we refuse to let anyone bear false witness against their own humanity. I/we receive the abundant love enfolded in the sanctuary of beloved community.

EIGHT

To My Seasoned Saints

(People Ranging from Gen X to Boomers and Beyond)

A PARABLE FOR MY SEASONED SAINTS

By the time my brother and I were in grade school and junior high school, respectively, both of my matrilineal grandparents had retired from teaching in the public school system. We would go down to Greenwood, Mississippi, and spend slow and sticky, hot summers with them. Most days were quite boring—to some degree. As I shared earlier, my grandaddy ruled the TV even though he slept through every show he demanded we watch. And Grandma would be cooking and cleaning and keeping us entertained as best she could. Unlike my grandfather, my granny had a penchant for staying busy and being on the move.

Some of my fondest memories include staying up late with my grandma as she told me stories from her past and rummaged through random old junk in her drawers and cedar chest looking for God knows what. I would lie on the right-hand side of her full-sized bed fighting off sleep and she'd sit on the left-hand side busying her hands and flapping her gums with funny memories. At the time, I listened intently, laughed from my belly, and slept so peacefully after listening to more than my fair share of her recollections of her youth. But now . . . I reach back into those memories we shared and peel back a layer of nuance that I was too young to understand then. I'm not sure I'd go as far as saying my grandmother suffered from some form of anxiety that disallowed her to sit still. But it would be many, many years and a serious hip injury before I would ever really see her sit down and just rest.

I think lots of compiling factors contributed to my granny's predisposition toward work and productivity. My grandfather was almost twenty years her senior and required lots of care in his aging years. My grandmother had also worked tirelessly to get herself off the sharecropping enterprise where her parents lived, going from picking cotton to putting herself through all her schooling and obtaining not just a bachelor's but also a master's degree— all while being a mother and a wife. There was never a time when the concept of "work" didn't signal some sort of freedom in my grandmother's purview. To be liberated from the grips of slavery and white supremacy meant that she would have to claw her way through sickness and health to get there. The same goes for my grandfather, who served in the military, fought in World War II, and used the GI Bill to put himself through college. He graduated when he was nearly forty years old.

Both of my grandparents had a grind-till-you-get-it mentality. And I remain grateful for the tenacity of all you elders I will forever lovingly call seasoned saints. Still. I see how that mentality has trickled down to younger generations (like myself, a proud geriatric millennial) and created some discord. From what I have been able to gather in my various spheres, the seasoned saints—people ranging from Gen X to boomers and beyond—often bring that same energy into relationships with younger folks. And, sometimes, it seems like y'all want us to labor and toil and grind all the time because that is, likely, what you have experienced for the better parts of your lives.

There are ways to push back against this legacy. In her digital platform The Nap Ministry, Southern-bred and seminary-trained Tricia Hersey cultivates a social media community that focuses on resisting the lie of constant grind-culture that results from oppression and capitalism. In her book *Rest Is Resistance*, Hersey offers a crucial reframe for that mentality:

> For Black people who are descendants of enslaved Africans via the Transatlantic Slave Trade and chattel slavery, consider the fact that your Ancestors built this entire nation for free with their stolen labor. Use this knowledge to tap into what they have already done, so you don't have to grind yourself into oblivion now.[1]

What is important for Bishop Hersey is that we all reconcile what systems of oppression have spoon-fed us about productivity and labor so that we might heal and actually be able to *sat down* somewhere and rest.

However, this movement for anti-oppressive rest seems to be going right over the heads of some of you seasoned saints and creating quite the generational divide. I've heard countless seasoned saints bemoan younger generations' work ethic, belittle their innovative ideas and energy, and be downright nasty upon any appearance of laziness or lack of deference. And more than it makes me mad, it truly makes me sad. Like my grandparents, many of the elders in our families and communities helped raise us and are vital members of our (chosen) tribe. But instead of seeing and supporting younger folks as they navigate the ever-evolving landscape of personal and professional achievement, it feels like y'all would rather fuss them into shame and submission. It is cruel and, what is more, unnecessary. But be clear: there is a necessary conversation that must be had with the younger crowd, too—which is why I've also included a letter to my young whippers and snappers later on.

The more I've wrestled with my own predilection toward constant productivity, the more I've had to get really honest about what it's attached to and how it is not serving me. And because I understand and believe in the principle of ubuntu (I am because we are), I am led to humbly offer grace and guidance to my seasoned saints. It does us no good to point fingers at whosoever generation has the most dysfunction. Rather, it would benefit all of us to endeavor to create tribe as sanctuary—especially in our intergenerational dialogues and relational dynamics. Here is what I offer as I speak directly to my elders: Lissen, y'all. It is okay to rest now. Much of the angst and anger you experience when dealing with younger people has less to do with whatever nonsense you think we/they are doing. And more to do with your lack of ability to trust that we/they are able to carry the loads you've carried. But here's the thing—you've done your work and fought the necessary fight so that the loads we carry are not the same ones you once wrestled to hold.

I say this from a deeply loving place because I am so deeply blessed to have been raised by a tribe of seasoned saints. And I also acknowledge the deep wounds of collective trauma surrounding productivity forced upon my ancestors who were subject to exploitative and violence-based labor—which was so integral to the capitalistic enterprise of slavery. Yet I am of the mind that the intergenerational conflict that we are facing can, and must, be overcome by intergenerational sanctuary that looks like making room for our varied lived experiences across time. Because no one in the younger generation wants to be disparaged for what we apparently lack (to older generations). Nor do I wish to minimize the sufferings or the strengths of those of you who came before us. For your labor has resulted in our reward.

All those times I stayed up late watching my grandmother toiling, rummaging through her old stuff, I never knew what she was looking for. But it strikes me now—I have found what she was looking for all that time. Tools and language and a way of being that allows me to rest. To be seated in contentment instead of stirred to busy-ness. That's the reward we gained for your indescribable and incredible sacrifices. Because, to put it plainly, I wouldn't have the tools or the language or the ability to rest if not for your willingness and our ancestors' willingness to go toe-to-toe with the very systems of oppression that required so much of you. You've fought white supremacy. You've fought gender discrimination. You've fought for systems to shape up and stand up to the task of what a democracy should truly mean. Those battles have resulted in changed realities for your offspring—your most treasured, sacred belongings. And that is a worthy recognition we should never take lightly.

It must also be said that younger generations are the material rewards that our deceased forebears never got to see or meet. We are indeed living their wildest dreams—your wildest dreams. And while there is elation at our arrival, perhaps some unsaid bitternesses choke you up from time to time. Many times, when I've experienced needless chastisement from a seasoned saint or another, I didn't hear correction. I heard sorrow. A hollow sadness perhaps because they've never experienced the life and opportunities that I've been given (or earned). None of that gives anyone license to stereotype or treat a person in another age group poorly. But it is a necessary truth that we must sit with as we consider what it means to create, do, or find sanctuary among one another.

Another African proverb says, *The youth may walk faster, but the elders know the way.* On the one hand, the saying is true and provides instructional value for youth to respect their elders. Yet I think the proverb is a bit narrow because I think there is a new world before us that none of us have seen. Not even y'all seasoned saints. And though you know the way (as the proverb says) to navigate it, that is not the *only* way, nor does it consider the new terrains of knowledge and skill that younger folks have developed. A mutuality of respect and honor will allow all of us to go farther—not necessarily faster—and together. This togetherness, the unwillingness to leave anyone behind, is the final facet of tribe as sanctuary that I pray every one of us understands.

A PRAYER FOR MY SEASONED SAINTS

God who loves across generations,

we thank You for the work of those who came before and
   for the bodily sacrifices of our elders.

We would not be who we are without their commitment
   to building a better life.

Forgive us, God, for the ways we have not honored their
   labor or remembered their love.

Give us wisdom to receive them with gentleness and
   grace—

and provide them room to experience that which has so
   long been denied.

Show us how to walk together into destinies of ease and
   joy and rest.

Because, like Your mercy, those are indeed our birth-
   rights—not just blessings we must work for.

Thank You for the opportunity to be held in the warmth
   of one another's hugs,

rather than experiencing more harm at one another's
   hands.

For sanctuary is what we desire and sanctuary is what we
   are determined to have.

Amen and ashé.

A PROMPT FOR MY SEASONED SAINTS

welcome

- How can we create intergenerational sanctuary? What
  truths need to be shared? What burdens need to be lifted?

- What legacies or unresolved traumas prevent you from
  truly resting?

- Who might you be (or who would you have been) if elder members of your tribe had been able to both rest and become their fullest selves?

witness

I have seen our grandmothers toil cleaning houses and
   feeding other folks' babies.
I have watched our grandfathers work odd jobs on top of
   their main jobs.
And I winced when I realized that their labor never
   earned them the material reward they deserved.
But hear me gently remind you: the predisposition
   toward labor was circumstantial, not cultural.
We do not have to view labor as a rite of passage.
We have a duty to reconcile what labor means given our
   present reality.
And I pray I will one day witness a new world where
   everyone's labor and lessons are respected and valued.

—love, Auntie.

writual

The call: I understand that it is easy to _____
(word meaning to direct) our dis-ease at the very people who
love us. And sometimes that causes _____
(word or phrase meaning conflict or hard feelings) where there
should be love, mutual respect, and wisdom-sharing. Today, I
strive to _____ (phrase meaning
to honor) the elders in my life as well as the generations coming behind me. Because I accept them as a _____
(word meaning needed or important) part of my chosen tribe
and see them as necessary for the sanctuary I deserve.

The response: I/we stand in agreement with the great cloud of witnesses whose love is diverse and divine. I/we support people in their fullness because I/we refuse to let anyone bear false witness against their own humanity. I/we receive the abundant love enfolded in the sanctuary of beloved community.

Porch Talk

"We All We Got" and Other Lessons from Traditional Communalism

Y'ALL READY TO JOIN ME ON THE PORCH TONIGHT? Auntie feels like she's said a whole lot, and now we need time to just let it all simmer. Because, baby, it's always appropriate to have a seat (and in some cases, several) and take a listen! So according to Auntie porch etiquette, we're gonna start with all the Tea first, then we will get into the honest-to-goodness Truth(s). Here's the tea (as in "oh, that'll *teach*" moments):

- Babies and fools: Those who don't know no better need hand-holding and a healthy dose of hard (but necessary) conversations to be made whole—but most folks throw them away because they lack the patience required to maintain a relationship with them.

- Beloveds: Those who show us a better way to do faith and community are likely the very people whom society deems unacceptable, unfit, or just plain old unkempt— and the gag is that they were Jesus' love language and among His first choice as disciples.

- Blessed hearts: Those who have been harmed or those who just do stupid stuff often suffer in silence because they fear rejection and have experienced the weaponization of their vulnerability.

- Seasoned saints: Those who are Gen X, boomers, and beyond are experiencing rising poverty and disconnection from family and community care especially since the start of the coronavirus pandemic; and while their methods may be antiquated, they still matter and deserve care.

Here's the unifying truth among these sometimes overlapping groups: Systems of harm and oppression wreak havoc on their sense of sanctuary while simultaneously fostering disconnection and distrust among those who otherwise might be part of their chosen tribe. And because we often give in to believing societal scripts that cast these people in the worst or most negative light, we end up reinscribing our own prejudices and projections onto them. It's cyclical and unrelenting. What we don't understand or fear about them becomes the only thing we look for and is proven by confirmation bias rather than actual relationships with them.

Several years ago, Nigerian writer Chimamanda Ngozi Adichie gave a TEDx talk entitled "The Danger of a Single Story." She recounts her experience going to college and meeting her roommate. Her roommate had all sorts of unrealistic expectations about her—such as her listening to only African tribal music or not speaking English. "She had felt sorry for me even before she saw me," says Adiche in her speech.

> Her default position toward me, as an African, was a kind of patronizing, well-meaning pity. My roommate had a single story of Africa: a single story of catastrophe. In this single story there was no possibility of Africans being similar to her in any way, no possibility of feelings more complex than pity, no possibility of a connection as human equals.[1]

The problematic single story phenomenon that Adichie out-lines is a bit like what I'm suggesting. We all have the ten-dency to single-story people with whom we have ideological oppositions, adversarial relationships, or are just simply mis-understanding. The single story is compounded when those people also happen to have varying views—which might even include harmful beliefs and practices—that make it even eas-ier for us to cast them aside as too problematic. Yet rarely do we peel back the layers of oppression and interconnected ide-ologies like capitalism, white supremacy, patriarchy, and so on in order to see the multitude of stories that uphold the very system that has produced the problems we are all navigating. So we operate with walls and wariness where we should be trying to figure out how to offer warmth and welcome.

Let me clear something up before you get the wrong idea. Auntie is not telling you to have a perpetual soft spot for peo-ple who are toxic and unyielding perpetrators of harm. You should never feel led to place yourself in a position where your safety or sanctity is threatened. However, I want us to sit with what it would mean to try a little harder to build the exact opposite of what we know as "cancel culture," where folks pub-licly oust, ostracize, or shun a person who has done something socially unacceptable or harmful. Cancel culture is typically aided by social media and has resulted in people being fired, fined, and even assaulted. So often, we allow cancel culture to permeate our interactions with people like my babies and fools, beloveds, blessed hearts, and seasoned saints. But I believe they are worth the trouble of trying to call them into sanctuary rather than call for their cancellation.

The womanist tenet of traditional communalism illumi-nates how "the practical wisdom and common sense of Black women support the survival and success of the Black community."[2] Essentially, it is a way of interacting with others, interceding on their behalf, and engaging in the work of accountability and wholeness. It's my favorite of the four tenets. Traditional communalism highlights the significance of community and the collective well-being in Black women's lives. It stresses the interconnectedness of individuals within the community and the importance of communal support systems. This tenet values the wisdom, practices, and traditions passed down through generations, recognizing the role of community in sustaining and nurturing individuals, especially Black women. In all the ways that white dominant culture entices us to focus on self, traditional communalism gives us spaciousness to stretch our hands outward to the safety found in community.

In the context of sacred belonging, I believe that *tribe is sanctuary* because it inspires us to push past disinterested critique—which makes cancel culture so pervasive—and invites us to step into a faith-filled commitment of determined connection and relationship with people who, quite frankly, need our help. Because if all we ever manage to do is call out people who are wrong or problematic, I think we risk losing touch with the fullness of our own humanity. Shame and submission are not the best tools we have to build the beloved community we deserve.[3]

Tribe as sanctuary, then, becomes our worthy and rightful task if we are to begin to heal together and build a more just and joy-filled world. This task is more than just replacing call-out / cancel culture with call-in culture—which seeks to invite someone to sit with the harms they've caused within community. Rather, I suggest pairing the commitment to tell the truth and speak truth to power with and among people whom you love and desire to hold accountable. It is what Auntie will call "wade-in" culture—going the extra step into somewhat murky waters for the sake of sanctuary and helping deliver someone to the other side of the shore. Take Miriam, for example. She waited by the shore of the Nile to see where her baby brother Moses would end up. Her actions were worthy and commendable. And because she stayed to keep watch, she was able to think fast and orchestrate her own mother's reconnection with Moses even while he was under the care of the pharaoh's daughter.

But what might have happened if Miriam had waded into that water *with* Moses? Perhaps her life would have been jeopardized for protecting her baby brother despite Pharaoh's edict to kill all the Hebrew-born boys. Still—what if her willingness to wade in on Moses's behalf would have given Miriam the chance to convince the princess that his life was worth saving while he was raised at home and among his biological family?

Of course, we will never know the answer to that question. Yet I wonder if my theological imagination might allow me the privilege to trouble you for just a little longer with this question: Whom would you wade into the waters of discomfort and uncertainty for? And what would you do to keep someone you cared for safe—so that you both might experience sanctuary together? If Miriam had waded in, Moses might have avoided being raised in the palace of his oppressors. If we were brave enough to wade in, countless others might be rescued from the grips of practices, people, and places who mean them harm.

I know what you may be thinking. And, sure. Not everyone in your atmosphere is going to be someone you'd wade in for.

But I can think of at least one or two people for whom I wish I'd waded in. Like the young boy (now man) in my church youth group who wrote me a long letter to confess that he was gay, and that he didn't want to be that way and go to hell. I, having no seminary education or real tools to respond better at the time, distanced myself and resorted to offering him my prayers that he would be delivered from the "lifestyle" of homosexuality. He doesn't go to church anymore now that he is a grown man and (from what I can see on social media) living his best life. If I'd had the courage to wade in, even without all the tools and the learning I have now, I might have been able to be a supportive corner and safe space for him as he figured out who he was. He might have never left the church. He might even have helped me become a better Christian and minister sooner (not that it would have been his responsibility to do so as the person most vulnerable and in need of support). Still. If I had waded in for him, things might be different for the both of us.

To create sacred belonging and commit to tribe as sanctuary is to recognize that when we build our chosen family or village of support with intention, it often results in life-giving, life-affirming relationships akin to divine places of safety. It is to live into the call to be(come) sources of refuge for ourselves and others who otherwise would not experience care, inclusion, or welcome. It is to wade in with courage and wisdom when all others have forgotten, or forsaken, Jesus' call to love thy neighbor as thyself.

Wonderful for us that we have historical and deeply relevant examples of those who know what it means to wade in and build tribe as sanctuary. One such example is Fannie Lou Hamer—legendary foremother of the civil rights movement.

She was what Auntie would call a No-Limit Soldier (in the words of Master P)—a strategic community organizer who not only helped spearhead the Freedom Democratic Party in the mid-1960s but also constantly put her life on the line to register other residents of Mississippi to vote in a time when Black people were being lynched for doing so. She would not simply hope that people made it to the courthouse to register. She would wade in those troubled waters and go with people to register, acting as a shepherd and a friend.

We can also look to fictional character Shug Avery—as conceived in Alice Walker's 1982 novel (now Broadway musical and films) *The Color Purple*. While Shug may seem a complicated character to some, for the novel's protagonist, Celie, she was a savior. Celie knew nothing but brutality, cruelty, and violence from the hands of her father and husband. But Shug came along and introduced her to intimate love, the beauty of God and nature, and her own agency and desires. And because of Shug, Celie broke free of her hellish captivity, reclaimed a relationship with her long-lost sister and children, and built a life filled with abundance and joy. Shug waded in for Celie. And Celie came out on the other side a new woman, more whole and magnitudes more free. Shug was Celie's person. Her God-ordained tribe. And the unapologetic permission and safety found in their relationship is the sanctuary all of us deserve.

The last example I will point to is the musician Lizzo. Lizzo took the music and entertainment industry by storm and offered much needed room and attention for Black women (and people of all genders) to center celebration and positivity with songs like "Truth Hurts" and "Good as Hell." Her music videos and tours have become a blueprint for intentional inclusion for the LGBTQIA+ community, self-avowed fat women who are unabashedly and unapologetically pushing back against European beauty standards as the curvy and bodacious baddies that they are, and other underrepresented people in the industry. Additionally, when she was called-in by people in the disability community concerning song lyrics that were offensive and derogatory, Lizzo course-corrected and changed the song immediately.

Lizzo is also a noteworthy example of how even in our attempts to be inclusive, we can still cause harms and be subject to necessary accountability. The public lawsuits filed by her former dancers alleging a hostile work environment prove that. But while Lizzo may not be perfect, her way of building community and creating tribe is something we can consider for sacred belonging. For many, Lizzo made it okay to be loud, proud, fat, or queer. With her insistence upon bold authenticity, she fashioned together a sanctuary that many have never experienced (especially in church). And with lots of effort, a whole bunch of unlearning, and a generous helping of humility, it's possible for us to do it too.

Because everyone looks at platonic and familial relationships differently, let's talk about what it might look like for us to take the work of creating tribe as sanctuary. I offer a few tips at the end of this section, but I suggest you first begin by defining "tribe" for yourself. What makes a chosen tribe different from, or similar to, a biological family? Think about the kind of communication and interactions your ideal chosen tribe would have. Begin to actually envision what it would mean for you to have a chosen tribe with which to do life. And second, ask yourself how you imagine it should feel to be held in a true sanctuary. Perhaps you've never had a space where you felt truly safe, seen, or understood. What would it mean, then, to relentlessly pursue the feeling of sanctuary with your close friends and relationships?

If you're stuck or having a little trouble answering these questions, it's okay. I'll go first. For me, tribe is like having a consistent group of people who make it their duty to say "Sawubona," which means "I see you." Tribe is taking the saying *we all we got* and putting hands and feet to it so much that when life starts life-ing, tribe shows up with mutual aid, collective care, and an abundance of emotional support. And sanctuary . . . well, that one is even easier for me to describe. Sanctuary tastes like the most delectable spinach soup my coworkers brought for me when grief—after the sudden passing of my bonus dad— had pushed me to the brink of starvation. Sanctuary is the Big Sisters of my sorority coming to look for me when I was feeling depressed during college. Sanctuary is the firm but necessary corrections from people who actually cared enough to stop me from causing harm to myself or others.

I'll go a step further and talk about how crucial it is for us to consider tribe as sanctuary a necessary, systematic tool for thwarting the tricks of evil and white supremacy. Think back to the Underground Railroad—that network of safe houses and abolitionists who worked together clandestinely alongside folks like Harriet Tubman was able to liberate multitudes of enslaved Black people. The Underground Railroad is a relevant example of how tribe as sanctuary isn't just about individual comforts or singular relationships. It is very much about building coalitions and networks of activism, advocacy, and aid such that oppression cannot make itself at home among the most vulnerable or our loved ones. As Reverend Mother Teresa rightfully reminds us:

Let us not use bombs and guns to overcome the world. Let us use love and compassion. Peace begins with a smile. Smile five times a day at someone you don't really want to smile at; do it for peace. Let us radiate the peace of God and so light His light and extinguish in the world and in the hearts of all men all hatred and love for power. Today, if we have no peace, it is because we have forgotten that we belong to each other—that man, that woman, that child is my brother or my sister.[4]

We are, indeed, one another's sacred belongings. Thank you, Mother Teresa, that even as you are now in that great cloud of witnesses, your words and wisdom still bear witness to what God calls each of us to do.

It's hard to top the iconic Mother Teresa, so Reverend Auntie is going to wrap this here porch talk on up. But, as promised, I want to offer a few tips for beginning the journey toward creating your own tribe as sanctuary. I pray that they bless you and challenge you to keep trying, even if you don't get it the first time.

Tip 1: Co-create rules of engagement with your chosen tribe so that sanctuary is not only realizable but remains sacred and respected. No one gets to desecrate what you and your tribe have worked so hard to create. And everyone gets to contribute to the vitality and vibe of the safe space you all have labored to bring to life.

PRO TIP: Investigate the differences between calling-in and calling out. Shifting your frame of reference will help you be a better human and tribe member.

Tip 2: Understand that tribe is not always static or rigid like a building or structure. Rather, tribe shifts with our evolution and our (un)becoming. In some seasons of life, your tribe may seem especially tight; other times, you will enjoy the company of added friends in your circle. Either way, flow like water and be amenable to how your chosen tribe shifts, shrinks, goes, and grows.

PRO TIP: Create a prayer or ritual of welcome and release to enable you to accept the varying iterations of your tribe over time. I promise it will help.

Tip 3: Dare to be fully yourself with your tribe. It's easy to compartmentalize or hide parts of ourselves—especially when dominant society has labeled us as a problem in some way. But we deny ourselves safety and refuge when we hide who we are from those who love us. Embracing our whole selves in the presence and protection of our posse will loose us from the demons of self-deprecation and open us to experience the world with more joy and delight.

And whatever you do, dear ones, always remember to wade in the water . . . wade in the water for all the blessed hearts. Wade in the water for the babies and the fools. Wade in the water for the beloveds. Wade in the water for the seasoned saints too.

> Wade in the water.
> Wade in the water, children.
> Wade in the water.
> God's gonna trouble the waters.
> —love, Auntie.

SACRED BELONGING COMMITMENT #3

Tears Are Salvific Work

And a woman in the city who was a sinner, having learned that he was eating in the Pharisee's house, brought an alabaster jar of ointment. She stood behind him at his feet, weeping, and began to bathe his feet with her tears and to dry them with her hair, kissing his feet and anointing them with the ointment. . . . Therefore, I tell you, her many sins have been forgiven; hence she has shown great love. But the one to whom little is forgiven loves little." Then he said to her, "Your sins are forgiven."

—Luke 7:37–38, 47–48

I praise you, for I am fearfully and wonderfully made.
Wonderful are your works; that I know very well.

—Psalm 139:14

I found God in myself & I loved her . . . fiercely.

—Ntozake Shange, For Colored Girls Who Have
Considered Suicide/When the Rainbow Is Enuf

NINE

To My Sugas

(People Who Are Fragile and Flamboyant, Awkward and Awesome—aka Neurodivergents)

A PARABLE FOR MY SUGAS

Some of my earliest memories are of people I love mocking me or cheering me on—it's hard to distinguish the two now.

> *She talk so proper like.*
> *Say it again so they can hear how you talk.*
> *Read it out loud—since you talk so good.*

I never knew whether to be proud of myself for speaking the way my mother and father also spoke. Or whether to be ashamed.

Ashamed of how "whiteness" showed up in my voice and made my subjects and verbs agree, even when I wished they didn't. Or how it tricked the Black girls at school into believing I wanted to be white. Or when it obscured the other dialects I could speak and understand fluently because my tongue was trained in it so well.

It never seemed to matter that I always understood people who looked like me—no matter where they came from or how many books they could read. Because even though I was just as at home listening to the cadences of African American vernacular, growing up I was always met with the suspicion that I couldn't possibly understand or carry on a conversation using AAVE.

It has only taken me some thirty-odd years to be okay with people's perplexed reading of me. The constant nagging posture of questioning that screamed in a whisper, "Who is this awkward Black girl and why does she talk so white?"

It never made any sense to me.

That I, a chocolate little Black girl with thick, coily hair and a Kenya doll clad in kente cloth could be talking "white." And what did that even mean? How does anyone who is Black bodied and raised in the American South, with its vestiges of segregation and slavery, speak the language of their oppressor? And why did my way of speech turn into a weapon against my own kin when all I ever wanted to do was be loved by them?

Let me unequivocally say: it is no light or laughing matter to lob an accusation of whiteness onto someone living in a Black body. To say it, even in jest, is to undercut the essence of every experience that makes that person Black.

Because, if there's one thing I've learned in all these years in my body, it is that Blackness is not merely a color, nor is race just an ethnic designation. Being Black comes with some show-and-tell. Being Black means showing your self (your skin) as only partial proof of your identity and being able to tell the truth, and the difference, of what is authentic to the Black experience. But oftentimes, in my own life, it was never safe to get outside of the bounds of what was considered Black enough to be a part of the Black experience. There was a constant push and pull of knowing in my body that I was untouchable (by whiteness) because I was Black but that I was also not fully seen by my Black peers.

Just as I endured the shaming of my white teacher in grade school, I faced a constant refrain of suspicion or second-best from white people, students and teachers alike, as I matriculated into high school. While I had a couple of white friends who played sports with me, I always felt like an afterthought to the main act of their evolving friendships and popularity. Even more devastating was my fate with the Black kids at school. Between the snide remarks about my perceived snobbery or downright rudeness and jokes about the way that I spoke, I did not have a good rapport with many of the Black students I would have loved to get to know. Sadly, all I had was a seeming never-ending sea of whiteness looking back at me, and I was unable to find a place to truly belong.

So, my body learned to monitor and adjust. Adapt and compartmentalize from a very early age. I learned that I needed to be quieter in spaces where there were more Black kids than usual. Clearly, I could not give them any more ammunition or fodder to make fun of me or shoot me down with their mockeries. Instead, I people-watched—almost longingly—while in their presence and secretly prayed that some other poor soul would be the object of their scrutiny that day. Most disheartening, however, was the way I learned to laugh at my pain whenever I became the butt of a joke.

> *She always got that white girl voice.*
> *That's cuz she know she wanna be white.*

My body learned how to cover up the harm and find it humorous, even at my own expense. Good or bad, one of the hallmarks of Black identity is being able to take a joke. So, of course, I had to show that I had the ability to perform my Blackness—even if others didn't accept me as such and even if I had to laugh to cover up my silent tears.

Conversely, I quickly intuited that most white people, while nice, were generous in their sharing only because they wanted to keep a close watch on how well I was doing. This was necessary because they wanted (or needed) to have a leg up on me, and they always found small ways to attempt to bring me down a ladder rung or two if I got too close to their achievements. It was always there. The not-so-subtle resentment that I had experienced with my third-grade teacher was an ever-present undercurrent in my dealings with most of my white peers. I never wanted them to get too comfortable with attempting to dim me. So my body learned how not to shine too bright whenever I was around them.

In hindsight, it was such a limiting time of my life that I often marvel at how I survived. The one saving grace was that, in all my compartmentalizing and bracketing and suspending parts of myself given my circumstances, I *always* knew who I was. I was the kid who loved musicals and also gospel music (namely, the Mississippi Mass Choir). I was the kid who went to HBCU football games to see the battle of the bands and enjoyed sci-fi books. I was the kid who loved to sit down with my grandma and shell peas and also had no problem sitting alone while writing my own short stories or reading comics. I was the kid who always knew how proud I was to be Black and that the features of my identity were not always welcomed or understood. I knew, and still do, where I am free to be all that I am.

When I look back over that time in my life, I lovingly name myself and all others who, like me, were just as awkward and awesome and fragile and flamboyant and likely neurodivergent, too, as my sugas. There is an innocent sweetness that I managed to carry with me through all those lonely, hellish years. A sensitivity to myself and to being misread and misunderstood that caused me to cry quite a lot during that time in my life. Sometimes I would lock myself in my room and just cry inexplicably. I also remember crying to my mother one day in elementary school when I realized why certain kids were ostracized and had no friends (they were classified as special ability students, and some of them had diagnoses such as Down syndrome). My heart literally ached with pain when I realized that people didn't see them as "normal" or worthy of friendship. Their loneliness at school was palpable, and I understood it, deeply, in an embodied way. My mom probably chalked up my emotionality to my going through puberty and being overly hormonal. And some of that could be attributed to my changing body. But, in hindsight, I ascribe a large portion of it to the way my body already knew that tears are salvific work.

There is something radically and redemptively healing about tear-work. Especially when it is the last, perhaps most sacrificial, offering you have when you have nothing else. In Luke 7, we meet a woman who lies at Jesus' feet and anoints them—washing them with her tears. If we use our theological imaginations for a moment, we must contend that the woman must've been crying profusely in order to have enough tears to wash perfume from Jesus' feet. We know nothing else from the text other than that the Woman Who Loved Much (as I prefer to call her, since we never learn her name) had a few sins and griefs to bear. Some like to speculate as to the nature of her sins. However, I've been taught to read biblical texts and contexts while considering the unique plight of marginalized women. This womanist hermeneutic of suspicion* asks me to imagine that perhaps her sins weren't bad deeds against others. Maybe they were harms she was carrying that caused her to suffer from self-doubt, self-loathing, or self-hatred. The wounds she harbored were enough to inflict deep pain. A pain that pushed her tears to the surface in an endless stream. Jesus chastises the Pharisee who wanted to eschew the woman's presence. He takes notice of how much the woman has shown love and forgives her of all her sins. Immediately, and on sight of her vulnerability, Jesus provides her the healing she likely never thought she'd receive.

This is my premise for the third theological commitment of sacred belonging: *tears are salvific work.* Our bodies often know the way to save us, and our tears call forth that healing on a soul level—sometimes even before we realize that we have a wound that needs tending. I say this because my teary sensitivities in my younger years were often the unspoken prayers that I wasn't self-aware enough to pray on my own but still needed God to hear. For all the times I was read as goofy, picked on for characteristics I truly couldn't help, I absorbed those rejections as proof that I was deficient. But my tears would not let that be my truth. Instead, they were the rallying cries that called Jesus into my heart and allowed miracle-working power to begin ministering in those crevices of pain. Tears were the warriors fighting to provide care for those tender places. Tears were my reminders—inner landscape markers that brought me back home to myself. The good creation that had always been fearfully and wonderfully made by an almighty God.

I pray that we all come to experience this redemptive act of salvific work. Whether we are struggling with exhausting all avenues in pursuit of self-acceptance, subject to external oppressions that take us to our brink, or maybe just walking through an extremely difficult season of hardship and grief—we all deserve to know that we are good creation, beloved by God.

A PRAYER FOR MY SUGAS

God who made us with no mistakes,
we praise You for how we are known by our names—
that no part of us is unseen or unloved by You.
Help us, Holy One, to fully recover from the wounds of
those we long to be loved by.
And give us strength to reclaim the beauty of who we are
when we've buried it deep inside.
Show us the way to unearth our vulnerabilities, that our
tears may water the seeds of Your saving power in us.
May we ever know the radical and revolutionary nature of
Jesus' healing in all the places where we store our pain.
Let salvation be a work we willingly participate in, for
as long as it takes for us to love ourselves as sacred
belongings.
Amen and ashé.

A PROMPT FOR MY SUGAS

welcome

- When was the last time you had a good, long, and necessary cry? What precipitated it—and did you invite God into that sacred and vulnerable space with you?

- What are things you've been taught—whether cultural or spiritual beliefs—that made you feel the need to compartmentalize or hide parts of yourself? What have you done with those parts of you?

- What is your definition of salvation? Is it a one-time event? Does it require your participation? How might you begin to adjust your view on the function of salvation as something you actively participate in?

witness

I have seen how oppressive voices drown out your truth.
I have watched you fold yourself neatly into envelopes
    assigned to you.
And I know you are tired of being what everyone else
    expects of you—
all the while being yourself is never enough.
I pray that you will stop the charade and ask: What do I
    believe about myself?
For it is in asking yourself to be yourself
that you will find your strength and your voice.
    —love, Auntie.

writual

The call: I recognize that I have not always been _____
(phrase meaning to be authentic), because of how others

view me. And I no longer want to participate in my own
_____ (phrase meaning demise or self-hatred).
From this point forward, I make it my intention to embrace
_____ (phrase referring to parts of your-
self that you once ignored or felt the need to hide).

The response: I/we stand in agreement with the truth that we
are all fearfully and wonderfully made. I/we value the fullness
and uniqueness of your lived experiences and affirm that all
of who you are matters to God. I/we support the healing journey you are on, as we offer our tears of joy for the saving work
God is doing in your life and tears of sorrow for all that you
have suffered as well.

TEN

To My Niblings

(Transgender, Nonbinary, and Gender-Fluid People)

A PARABLE FOR MY NIBLINGS

Put her in ballet, she thought.

Yeah, that's what I'll do.

And that's exactly what my mother did. As I described earlier, my mother put me in ballet from about age six to eight. I was tall and slender and energetic. The perfect candidate for dance class. I do not think my mother was trying to train the tomboy out of me. But it was around that time I began to understand that I was not like all the prissy, prim, and proper girls at school. I wasn't "unladylike," as the elders used to call it, on purpose. More like, I was aggressive and athletic and didn't always know how to exude gracefulness with my body. So even though my mother never said as much to me, I began to interpret my time in dance school as a means to soften me up a little.

Too bad, the lessons never took. I was the most awkward and eager little ballerina in that class. Too forceful for the moves, I bounded and leaped through the choreography like a basketball power forward (the position I ended up playing later in life . . . go figure) rather than a smooth and effortless gazelle like the others. It was a prophecy that I'd never escape. For years after—even well into my thirties—people would comment on my athletic build, my slender but muscular frame, and even the way I walked. I tend to have a stiffness to my gait, which is a genetic and learned behavior from my dad, from whom I take my height and build. And for the world around me, the way that I carried myself was considered not feminine enough. How I presented in my body (my walk, etc.) seemed to be the driving force in the most strange and uncomfortable interactions.

So, you used to play ball, right?
Do you date? Oh, really . . . I didn't think you would have a
    boyfriend.
You like girly things?

The questions, in and of themselves, were not the problem. It was the constant and nagging suspicion that something about me was a problem. I found resonance with this experience as I sat down with a pastor friend of mine who is nonbinary (and who uses they/them pronouns). As my friend began to talk me through their experiences of feeling like an outsider in their own body because of their parents' and grandparents' expectations of how they should behave or show up, I realized that the cognitive dissonance I felt when met with such accusatory and probing questions was not that

I was ashamed of who I was. Rather, it was that the world had some other determinations of who I should be.

I do not tell this story to draw attention to my own feelings. However, it is important to me to draw parallels with my lived experiences as a point of entry to the unique and complex experiences of people who are transgender, nonbinary, or gender-fluid. I have been blessed to sit with and learn alongside some of the most amazing thinkers and people of faith while in seminary. Some of them happened to also be transgender and nonbinary. As they befriended me and invited me to get to know them, I found that most of them had reconciled that gender (and gender construction . . . because gender is often created and reinforced by societal rules) is more closely aligned with a spectrum rather than a binary. Sure, in toddler terms, one might think of someone as either being male or female as proven by their anatomical design. But gender is far more complex than that. As a matter of fact, every person alive has a unique makeup of both testosterone and estrogen—the hormones that aid in reproduction and healthy bodily functioning. Does this mean that a man who has a higher occurrence of estrogen in his body than other men is "less of a man"? No, of course not. It just means that he is fearfully and wonderfully made. Regardless.

My pastor friend told me about how they struggled deeply with doubt and fear once they'd come to terms with who they were. They didn't want to let down their parents or the church people who had helped raise them by confessing the truth about their identity. But they could not erase the discomfort they felt when forced into a dress for church or asked to wear long hair and fingernail polish. The performance of gender roles based on what other people assign to us as "normal" or acceptable is the place where nonbinary people die silent deaths more often than we care to admit. Because just as we'd likely never ask a passionate basketball player to give up the game they love to practice ballet instead, we should never ask someone to deny who they are—especially when it is only to make others more comfortable. To ask a ball player to do that would signal a death of their very essence. And, unfortunately, I've seen far too many of my niblings experience deaths like that at the hands of the most well-meaning (but sometimes not) Christians.

What I hate even more than this bitter reality that many niblings experience is the constant weaponizing of the Bible to "justify" beliefs, behaviors, and even laws concerning transgender, nonbinary, and gender-fluid people. Here's a news flash: the closest (and I don't mean this to be reductive) thing we have in the Bible to transgender or nonbinary people is the mention of eunuchs. Named in both the Old Testament and the New, eunuchs do not fit into the standard male/female categories and point to a so-called different gender status. And while its not a perfect analog to the experiences of modern-day transgender or nonbinary people, eunuchs offer a glimpse into the reality that they are valued by God and were integral to God's purpose as Lover and Creator of all. That being said, it is enraging that Christian apologists and Bible-thumpers alike use literalist readings of Scripture to attempt to render my niblings invisible or their bodies as problems—when Jesus Himself consistently offered love and welcome to *all* people.

This is why Auntie wants to be so careful and more than certain to ask us to consider: What do we really mean by salvation? In Christocentric spaces and circles, salvation is the ultimate goal of all our doings as Christians. We are to go out and share the good news of Jesus so that others, by hearing the gospel message, would accept Jesus into their hearts and be saved. This form of salvation is wholly concerned with saving people from eternal damnation and fiery hell (for those who believe in it). Yet it has always troubled me that we get so fixated on a heavenly destination for our souls that we ignore the present reality for our bodies. Wouldn't salvation be all the more promising to people (as in, inviting for un-saved or nonbelievers) if we were just as concerned with creating pockets of safety for people who don't fit into the status quo? And what is so healing or salvific about disparaging someone's body to death—both literally and figuratively? Let me remind you that transgender youth and teens are more than seven times more likely to attempt suicide than other youth and teens.[1] And, for Auntie, just one consideration of death is far too costly for me. To be clear, this is not because there is something "wrong" with these children. When young people are supported by their families and communities, those rates drop significantly.

Here's what I know. While political pundits and pushy pastors are preaching anti-LGBTQIA+ rhetoric and complaining of indoctrination in our schools, I will weep for the children whose lives have been lost because we did not save them. Whether it's because we sat there, looking on in silence (read: complicity) as more of these young people suffered isolation, harassment, homelessness, and judgment. Or perhaps we believed all the hype and gave in to harmful narratives and beliefs about transgender people—voting people into office who have passed life-restrictive, death-dealing bills into law. Or maybe we wanted to do something to help, but in our ignorance, we did not know what to say or do. Hear me when I say, dear niblings: I am so sorry. Sorry for not seeing you. Sorry for contributing to your pain. Sorry for how you've tried to edit yourself like a backspace button when we should have cheered you on with an exclamation point. Sorry for not being brave enough to wade in the water and get a little muddy on your behalf. Sorry for not telling the truth and shaming the devil sooner. Sorry that we have failed you.

But that inactivity stops today. #NotOnMyWatch. The tears you have cried will not be in vain. I am hopeful that I, along with countless others, will aid in the salvific work your tears began and will stand up alongside you. Because today is the day we decide to work together in creating better, safer spaces for you. Here is where we can start (or continue) this theological commitment to treat all my niblings (transgender, nonbinary, and gender-fluid people) as a sacred belonging:

- We can take inventory of those in our lives who have been impacted by anti-LGBTQIA+ aggression and legislation and connect with organizations (like GLAAD, PFLAG, the Human Rights Campaign, etc.) to learn about ways to support them.

- We can become familiar with current terminology and inclusive language as well as cease all use of derogatory, problematic, and antiquated terminology. We can also help others learn the suitable vocabulary as allies (see a list of resources on the National Center for Transgender Equality website).

- We can funnel and redirect resources (such as funds, direct services, and other forms of mutual aid and collective care) to organizations and families who work to provide cover and support to transgender and nonbinary youth.

- We can learn about the unique experiences of BIPOC transgender, nonbinary, and gender-fluid persons, who are often prone to higher levels of violence and oppression because of their race and other intersectional identities.

The lesson of history that all human rights are indivisible and that the failure to adhere to this principle jeopardizes the rights of all is particularly applicable here. A built-in hazard of an aggressive ethnocentric movement which disregards the interests of other [marginalized] groups is that it will become parochial and ultimately self-defeating in the face of hostile reactions, dwindling allies, and mounting frustrations.[2]

—Rev. Dr. Pauli Murray,
"The Liberation of Black Women"

A PRAYER FOR MY NIBLINGS

God who made us in Your image,
thank You that every person You created is worth the same—worthy of tenderness and care.
God, we praise You for the manifold blessings that all LGBTQIA+ people are to the kin-dom.
For they are incarnate proof of the diversity of Your creative power.
Let us continue to see them, support them, and celebrate them where they are—while we strive to fight with them for the kind of world all of us deserve.
Help us, oh God, to heed their cries for care and lamentations for the love that is due them.

Forgive us when we are complicit in causing harm or,
  worse, when we are the cause of harm.
And give us wisdom and strength to stand in the gaps,
  listen to their needs, and respond accordingly.
For it is our duty to steward all our neighbors as a sacred
  belonging—so that their tears can turn into salvific
  work.
Amen and ashé.

A PROMPT FOR MY NIBLINGS
welcome

- What beliefs about gender identity and sexuality were passed down to you? Were they damaging? Were they helpful in understanding the depth of complexity of what gender is? Why or why not?

- Make a list of LGBTQIA+ organizations and public-facing advocates or persons that you'd like to learn more about. What are some things you hope to learn from them?

- When or how have you been complicit in harm against LGBTQIA+ persons (particularly transgender, nonbinary, or gender-fluid people)? How can you make amends for that harm?

witness

I have seen how religious teaching has turned into
  trauma
that shames people for who they are and how they love.
But your body was not meant to bear the brunt of your
  own disapproval

nor carry the burden of others' disdain for the complexity of God's creation.

Be clear: your body is not to be interpreted as a source of sin.

Rather, it is a site for sharing in the fullness of God's creation.

Disavow yourself of needing to believe your body is a problem.

Sit with the truth that your body is good and the receptor of unlimited love.

And release the guilt that you've held on to because it was taught as the only way.

For you are the imago Dei, beloved. And I am a witness.

—love, Auntie.

writual

The call: I honor the various identities my body knows and _____ (word meaning to value or respect) the identities of others. I release myself from the need to _____ (phrase meaning to believe) the lie that all people are not made in the image of God. And I will start today with the commitment to _____ (word meaning see or affirm) the dignity and humanity of everyone.

The response: I/we stand in agreement with the truth that we are all fearfully and wonderfully made. I/we value the fullness and uniqueness of your lived experiences and affirm that all of who you are matters to God. I/we support the healing journey you are on, as we offer our tears of joy for the saving work God is doing in your life and tears of sorrow for all that you have suffered as well.

ELEVEN

To My Love-Makers

(People, Typically Women, Who Are Stereotyped as Promiscuous but Are Truly Just Self-Possessed)

A PARABLE FOR MY LOVE-MAKERS

When I was growing up in the Black Baptist tradition, our church had LifeWay on speed-dial and ordered all its Christian education resources from their franchise. Never mind the deeply conservative and white theologies espoused in most of their curricula. While I value the foundation and formative space of learning my church upbringing provided, I also question the problematic things I was taught there. For example, it was in church that I learned that people experiencing poverty were likely there because of personal choice and not interconnected sources of disenfranchisement. It was also in the church where I learned that all gay people were supposedly going to burn in hell—regardless of whether they had professed a belief in Christ. Lastly, and absolutely still just as sad, I learned that women are responsible for men's (poor) sexual behavior and that we must do everything to hide ourselves from tempting them to fall.

It is also within this hyper-religious context that I experienced some of the funniest things I could never have imagined. I'm thinking specifically of how my mother often refused to allow my brother and me to buy costumes or participate in many Halloween festivities. This is because Halloween was regarded as a demonic, pagan tradition in our home and would not be tolerated, or celebrated, in any way. Thank God my mother and stepdad weren't complete jerks about it. After we attended the harvest or hallelujah night at church, we were permitted to go trick or treating with the neighborhood kids. But the gag was, we had to go as ourselves or rummage through our closets and make up an outfit from clothing we already had. Well, the only suitable articles of clothing I could piece together made me look like either a hobo or some character from Huckleberry Finn—so none of the nice candy-givers ever knew who or what I was supposed to be. It was embarrassing. My momma didn't care. All she knew is her children weren't going out the house dressed up as no ghoul, no ghost, or any other devilish character. After all, Black parents and folks alike don't play about no witchcraft or evil spirits. So, yes—humility and a healthy sense of humor were necessary elements of proficiency one needed to grow up in a churched, Black household.

But between the church pew and home, Black kids—especially little Black girls—learn to play small, engage in figurative self-flagellation, and crouch in silence. Even worse, Black girls very often learn the soul-shattering language of shame at the hands of church leaders and pastors. I was around thirteen or so the first time a teenaged girl was forced to come up before the entire church and apologize for having "premarital sex." She was the daughter of one of the most popular ladies who ran the culinary committee at church. If I remember correctly, the girl had sex with a teenaged boy who attended the very same church (and he was the son of one of our most powerful deacons . . . don't mind me, I'm just being petty). Was he brought before the church to confess his sins and ask forgiveness? Nope. He was not. She cried and shuddered as she stood there that night at Bible study and was made to admit that she had been caught having sex. She made no eye contact with any adults except for when the pastor addressed her directly. She looked down or past everyone's gaze, almost dissociatively. She kept her answers to the fewest number of words she could. *Yes sir. No sir. I don't know, sir. I'm sorry and want God to forgive me.*

I wanted to be certain I'd never have to live with such shame. So I begged God to make me as "pure" as possible. I went all in with the *True Love Waits* curriculum (yes, from LifeWay) and took the purity pledge alongside the other youth and teens at the church. Within a few months of our pledge ceremony, I recall certain cisgender male ministers having *talks* with the boys who were "smelling themselves." Unlike the strict, zero-tolerance policies the girls were met with should anyone be assumed to be acting "fast," these boys were essentially told it was natural and normal for them to be horny all the time and that they should just make sure to use protection. God forbid they get anyone pregnant or contract a sexually transmitted infection. Never mind the vow of purity until marriage they'd all signed. I'm being facetious, but the glaring disparity between an expectation that boys were going to have sex and girls were not to give in to sexual advances made absolutely no sense. If "boys will be boys" meant that sex was included, then who the heck were they going to be having sex with? To give boys the pass to have sex, it was clearly implied that they would have sex partners. Just not church girls.

Furthermore, nowhere in the conversation about abstinence did anyone discuss anything other than heterosexual relationships in the context of marriage. First off, this pretended as if there weren't gay, same-gender loving people right there in the congregation. And it implied that everyone in the world would have the desire to or successfully get and stay married. (As if at least some of those pastors and ministers weren't cheating on their spouses or having children out of wedlock all while preaching purity to everyone else.) In 2022, *The Journal of Blacks in Higher Education* cited these staggering statistics about US marriage rates:

> 34.4 percent of Black men were married in 2021, compared to 28.6 percent of Black women. For Whites, 55.5 percent of men and 52.4 percent of women were married. More than 48 percent of all Black women and 51.1 percent of Black men had never been married.[1]

This means that for all the preaching about saving sex for marriage, only about one in four Black women will have that chance. Are they (the remaining 71.4 percent of Black women in the United States), then, to believe they are called to a life of celibacy? I don't know that God requires that kind of loneliness of us—particularly when so many of us already sacrifice far too much far too often. I'll admit. I still do not consider myself to be a fully sex-positive* Christian or faith-leader. (If, like me, you are new to the term *sex positivity*, it's basically a movement to embrace sexuality as a healthy part of the human experience. It emphasizes the importance of human agency, safe-sex options, and consent.) I tend to err on the side of caution and will likely teach my daughter to give herself time to mature and make wise decisions regarding her own sexuality. *All* abstinence is not bad. However, I pray that poorly interpreted, non-contextual scripture and dogmatic doctrines do not infiltrate her most formative years. As her mother, I will try my hardest to provide her with a healthy sense of sexuality as a sacred belonging that only she and God can navigate together.

But I digress. By now, you already know that I ended up leaving my childhood church because of my former pastor's refusal to acknowledge my call to ministry. However, the lessons the church had taught me, year over year over year, did not leave me. At least not without a fight. Case in point: despite my enduring love for fantasy books, I did not read Harry Potter until well into my twenties (after I left the church), even though the first book of the series was published when I was thirteen. Harking back to the fear that anything witchcraft related was "of the devil"—the same belief that forbade us from fully participating in Halloween—I literally abstained from opening myself to the wonderful world of make-believe magic. Just like I abstained from sex and any other appearance that I was even interested in boys. From childhood into adulthood, I learned to deny myself access to vital parts of my humanity and the unique interests that, in moderation, were harmless. It felt, and in many ways still feels, like church precipitated a delayed puberty for me and so many other girls groomed to be good church women. Girls who contorted themselves to fit an impossible ideal of perfection only to have it never pay off with the material or marital benefits that were promised to them.

It is so ironic to me that while the "true love waits" ideology was meant to teach us about giving and receiving love, it taught me more about fear and death than anything. Even more ironic? Those who managed to dodge the shame-culture as found in most evangelical church spaces are actually the ones who taught me a great deal about love and life. It was young women in college and my early twentysomethings friendships who gave me a proper sex education—discussing the ins and outs of birth control, the proper reproductive healthcare and wellness routines, and even the basics about lust and physical desire. And the more I got to know these folks—ones who had been called fast or hot in the pants—I came to know them not as troublemakers but as love-makers. You see, they had learned how to belong to themselves well before being subjected to harmful beliefs about sexual purity as something that belongs to God. And because of that, they were unlearned in the language of sexual shame with which I had become fluent.

It's taken me years to appreciate these women for being self-possessed enough to stand comfortably in their own bodily autonomy and sexual agency. And I can confirm that many of them were and are some of the most faith-filled people I ever met. Their capacity to view their sexuality as something to exercise with self-trust, consent, and accountability—rather than some object that God would punish them for—is the lesson I believe most "churched" folks need.

So let me say the quiet part out loud to be abundantly clear. We are not now, nor have we ever been, meant for such bifurcated deformation that requires us to behave our way into perfection. Especially not in the quest to be in relationship with God. I believe with everything in me that God desires us to be whole versions of our fullest selves, not self-mutilated fragments we present as holiness. In the words of Ntozake Shange, every single one of us must be willing to say, "I found God in myself and I loved her . . . fiercely."[2]

As for the young woman who was humiliated in the supposed sanctuary of my church—and all those who true-love-waited their way into shame and trauma—I weep for them. I weep for all of us. Who were told to close our mouths and our legs instead of learning how to open our hearts and trust that God would walk with us as we discovered who we were and what love did (or did not) feel like. I weep for the times that we turned up our noses at the girls who came up pregnant, treating them as lepers and not loved ones. I weep for how forced abstinence also made us targets for sexual predators who knew that the "church girls" were vulnerable—and sometimes succeeded. I weep for the theologies that continue to be preached that pressure girls and women into fear-based submission while demonizing our bodies at the same time.

Just as I weep for the sadness caused by toxic beliefs, I weep in joy for the liberated prophets who are already here and still to come. Those like Lyvonne Briggs, author of *Sensual Faith*, and Rev. Whitney Bond, who dedicates her scholarly work to reclaiming spirituality and healthy sexuality. I weep in joy for all who have been freed from the chains of religious oppression and unhealthy patterns of self-denial. And I rejoice in gratitude for the tears brought on by laughter—for the enjoyment of pleasure need not be relegated to sex but should be inclusive of the depth of all our senses.

May our collective tears show us the way back to ourselves, wash us new, and bring us home to our bodies as sacred belongings.

Our bodies are not entities outside of ourselves that we need to "beat into submission." . . . Our body-temples are divinely designed to restore themselves . . . and help us to indulge in soft sacred spaces where we are reminded that we are intrinsically worthy of love, concern, care, and pleasure.[3]

—*Lyvonne 'Proverbs' Briggs,* Sensual Faith

A PRAYER FOR MY LOVE-MAKERS

God who made us fearfully and wonderfully,
we praise You that nothing about us is a surprise to
  You—
and that You look at Your creation and call us good.
Help us, oh God, to honor the beauty of our fullness and
  experience love in our bodies.
Release us from negative and unnecessary modes of compartmentalizing ourselves—
so that we may acknowledge the magnitudes with which
  You designed us.
Give us wisdom to share ourselves with people who war-
  rant our affections.
And show us the proper way to have consensual, divinely
  orchestrated relationships.
May this be Your desire for us—to wholly experience
  sacred belonging as a bodily pleasure.
Amen and ashé.

A PROMPT FOR MY LOVE-MAKERS

welcome

- Have you (or women in your life) experienced shame associated with sex? When and how did that begin?

- Outline any church or faith-based teachings that you or your loved ones received about sex and sexuality. Then label each teaching—is it rooted in unrealistic and misogynistic self-denial or in love-affirming exploration of sexuality?

- What do you need to lament about your religious or familial upbringing that has caused you to abandon or even dislike parts of yourself?

witness

I have seen the ways true love has been co-opted and
    commodified.
To make it seem like eros love is something to be
    ashamed of—
and that romantic love is all there is; everything you
    should aspire to.
I've watched how girls and women have been made to
    feel that their wholeness . . .
relies on their capacity to be successful in finding
    marriage.
To that I ask: why deny yourself the pleasure of love you
    desire?
And why limit yourself to a singular strand of love?
For I am a testament to the resurrecting power that exists
    in all forms of love.
And I want to witness you walk in the lavish love you
    deserve.

                                 —love, Auntie.

writual

The call: I recognize the shame-based _____ (word mean beliefs or teachings) I received that have caused me or my loved ones to _____ (phrase meaning to deny or view oneself/themselves negatively). But now that I know better, I resolve it within myself to _____ (phrase meaning to reclaim or honor) the fullness of our humanity and the _____ (phrase meaning beauty or goodness) that we are meant to experience with and in our bodies. I will strive to _____ (phrase or word meaning divest) myself from harmful beliefs that require me to view my body as a problem.

The response: I/we stand in agreement with the truth that we are all fearfully and wonderfully made. I/we value the fullness and uniqueness of your lived experiences and affirm that all of who you are matters to God. I/we support the healing journey you are on, as we offer our tears of joy for the saving work God is doing in your life and tears of sorrow for all that you have suffered as well.

TWELVE

To My Brave and Brazens

(Generational Curse and Toxic Relationship Breakers)

A PARABLE FOR MY BRAVE AND BRAZENS

This letter is hard to write. As a millennial who loves Jesus and therapy, being committed to my healing has meant saying goodbye to some people—including some people who are family. Growing up in a Black household, I learned the very toxic trait that what happens in the family stays in the family. This belief means an allegiance to unhealthy patterns of covering for, or remaining connected to, harmful familial relationships and keeping that harm private, sometimes, by any means necessary. And if you combine that with a "family over everything" mantra that tends to accompany that belief, there is little room to negotiate unpacking years of generational trauma, dysfunction, and even abuse.

I do not have a large family. Between my brother and my small circle of cousins, there might be fifteen of us—counting both sides of my immediate family. Cousins grew up treated almost as siblings. And cousins of my parents were seen as aunts and uncles. Add to that the second marriages of our parents and the accompanying stepsiblings. I grew up with a blended but small family unit.

While I remember much from my younger years very fondly, as an adult I recall those sweet memories holding in tension great joy and deep sadness. For as much as we enjoyed taco nights at my aunt's house, long road trips to Disney, or traveling across the state for weekly basketball games, unsaid things and deeply harbored resentments have long since unraveled the bonds of some of those relationships in my later years. Where I once found safety and welcome, I now struggle to navigate feeling seen or truly known with certain members of my family. When I got serious about going to therapy a few years back, I also got serious about being honest about these "family secrets" that I'd never really spoken about. And the truth was that underneath the appearance of solid sibling-cousin-family rapport, there simmered bitter sibling-cousin-family rivalry and dysfunction. Some of it brewed and stewed in what could be boiled down to plain old jealousy or resentment. Other parts stirred the pot of trouble because of much more serious issues—including substance and physical abuse. Either way, as someone who was sensitive and more prone to emotional scarring, I began to unpack this subtle (but also very loud) dis-ease within our family. And it became almost impossible for me to stomach as I got older.

Between the constant digs or insinuations that I thought I was better than everyone else or the outright insults and making fun of me, I became extremely self-conscious about how I showed up with my family. I started to engage in code-switching and people-watching within my family, just like I'd learned to do at my predominantly white high school. Rarely, if ever, did I feel welcome to share who I was and who I was becoming. And even though I didn't feel quite so guarded around most of my family members, because they were comfortable *not* confronting the horrible behavior of a few serial offenders, I decided to distance myself from everyone. In hindsight, I wish that I had never made separation from loved ones my protection of choice. However, when you are in your early twenties, sometimes you don't know what you don't know. And at the time, I didn't know another way (because . . . what happens in the family stays in the family, remember?) to navigate what was a really hard space.

So I explored the healthiest way I knew to cope: I cried (a lot). Grieving the rupture of my sense of security—and likely, my sense of self—was the only way to get through the pain. When you go from feeling safe with your family to suddenly being the subject of discussion or dissension, it feels like a death. And that manner of death, alongside the undoing of such formative relationships, requires a sacrifice of tears as offering. I had (and still have) regular offerings of seemingly endless tears on the altar made out of my pillows or in my shower. Between talking to God and my therapist in an effort to make sense of what went wrong, I began to reconcile that many things can be true at once. The truths for me and my particular family were these:

- That our parents made decisions that had long-term con-sequences *on us* and never talked *to us* about them. Some

of those decisions were horrible and some of them resulted in lasting harm, but all those decisions were theirs to
make, and they tried the best they could at the time.

- We were (sometimes unknowing) carriers of our parents'
  pain and unresolved trauma—especially considering the
  vestiges of white supremacy, anti-Blackness, and class divisions that result when Black families are trying to claw
  their way out of poverty and oppression.

- I probably did come off as an entitled jerk during those
  years (from about age sixteen to twenty-fiveish, we all
  likely struggle with self-development). And I aggravated
  matters when I was not self-aware enough to realize it.
  Yet there is grace in realizing that I was very sheltered
  and well loved—which may have been an unforeseen
  trigger for family members who did not have the same
  safeties in their home lives.

- *Still*, how I experienced my family is valid. The toxicity
  that was permitted profoundly affected me and caused
  wounds from which I am still recovering.

But perhaps what's most important out of all this: I am now
brave and brazen enough to confront these generational
curses and toxic relationship patterns for the demons that
they are. And to these things—principalities, in the words of
Ephesians 6:12 (KJV)—I say: *Knuck if you buck* 'cuz I ain't
scared of y'all anymore.[1]

Prolific and prophetic Black feminist thinker Audre Lorde
gave me words for how I've cultivated the ability to face the pain
that still calls from my past. "There is a distinction," she writes,
"between pain and suffering."

Pain is an event, an experience that must be recognized, named and then used in some way in order for the experience to change, to be transformed into something else, strength or knowledge or action. Suffering, on the other hand, is the nightmare reliving of unscrutinized and unmetabolized pain. When I live through pain without recognizing it self-consciously, I rob myself of the power that can come from using that pain, the power to fuel some movement beyond it. I condemn myself to reliving that pain over and over . . . whenever something close triggers it. And that is suffering, a seemingly inescapable cycle.[2]

So much of our suffering leaves us in perpetual states of self-sacrifice and silence—carrying "unscrutinized and unmetabolized" pain around as a weapon we wield over others. And so many of the generational curses and toxic relationship patterns we find ourselves in are repeated cycles simply because we refuse to name and process what has happened to us, in us, and with us. But, beloved, we can't save ourselves from what we cannot stare down with the same vengeance with which it tried to swallow us whole. We will never free ourselves from the suffering if we are unable to face it down and fight it outright.

The theological commitment of tears as salvific work is but the first step in participating in the remedy for our internalized pain—particularly in our family dynamics. For all the times we were subjected to un-preferential or differential treatment, let the tears flow. For all the times we were judged for genetic characteristics that we could not change, let the tears flow. For all the times we were left unprotected or under the care of those who harmed us, let the tears flow.

For all the times we witnessed abuse and danger, seen and unseen, let the tears flow. For all the times we stuffed down our humiliation and covered it with humor, let the tears flow. For all the times we had our lives turned into grounds for competition and comparison, let the tears flow. And for all the time that has gone by—without recognition of the hole in our family or the hope of reconciliation—let the tears flow.

As the tears flow, I believe they will carve paths of truth-telling into the hardened soil of our hearts. And as our tears penetrate those hard places, seeds of courage will be watered and begin to show us that we can do hard things. For me, it looked like having difficult conversations with immediate family members. Some of those conversations yielded miraculous results. To have your father apologize for his absence and some of his unwise choices is—well, quite healing and powerful. And to forge new relationships with sibling-cousins estranged by strain and distance is an amazing gift that would not have happened without my committing to doing the hard thing.

Still. I will name that not all the conversations were perfect. I found that some family members were likely never going to listen to or acknowledge my version of events. Rather, they needed me to serve as the scapegoat for years of unmetabolized pain. But though my tears were met with resistance and refusal to see my heart, those encounters also washed me of the shame and guilt I'd felt for years. Having that hard conversation, and crying my way through it, both preserved and released me from continuing to contribute to the dysfunction. I am forgiven because, as in Luke 7 with the Woman Who Loved Much, Jesus said so. What's more, I am free because *I said so.* I refuse to be a victim of my trauma, generational curses, and toxic relationships any longer. And regardless of whether others choose to forgive me for things I've done wrong (and, yes, I did ask forgiveness), my liberation does not hinge on their capacity to do so.

Let me also hurry to speak directly to you, my fellow brave and brazens. It's okay if you never get to a place of having hard conversations with people who have harmed you. I am grateful that was my testimony. It may not be your story. But the good news is that your tears can still do salvific work by allowing you to confront the pain that lingers in your body and provide time for self-reflection about what to do next. For some of you, that might look like having hard conversations with the persons who have hurt you. For others of you, that could mean going to therapy, journaling, or writing letters to those parties that you keep for yourself. Either way, I invite you to explore tears as salvific work simply because you deserve to be free of the burdens you've been carrying. Allow your tears to train you in your body's native tongue— of talking to God when you don't have the words to say, telling you how to get back to who you are. Who you've always been. Fearfully and wonderfully made.

A PRAYER FOR MY BRAVE AND BRAZENS

God who loves all of who we are,
we thank You that we have the authority to confront
principalities and powers that harm us—
even when they exist in the places where we should be
safest.
Help us, oh God, to metabolize the pain so that we may
not proliferate the suffering.

> Show us how to weep for the wounds and war for our
> healing.
> For healing and wholeness is our sacred belonging.
> Amen and ashé.

A PROMPT FOR MY BRAVE AND BRAZENS
welcome

- Reflect on loved ones who have caused you great harm.
  Write out how what they did was unacceptable and the
  boundaries you will commit to keeping in light of those
  actions.

- Are there any faith practices or theologies that contribute to your ability, or inability, to address generational
  trauma or toxicity? Please spend time considering how
  and why.

- Have you seriously considered going to therapy? If you
  have not, will you try (pretty please—because your favorite Auntie asked)? If you have pursued therapy, have you
  seen a shift in your capacity to handle conflict? How so?

witness

> I noticed how family switched up on you.
> Discarded you and then deemed you the problem.
> I see how you carry that rejection with you.
> How your celebrations have been met with silence.
> And I know that it still hurts.
> But I am also a witness of your growth and goodness.
> Do not let their refusal to know you define you as deficient.
> Their incapability to see you is rooted in trauma—not
> truth.

So, free yourself of the desire to fix their view of you.
Because transgressing their toxicity is not, and has never
   been, your responsibility.

—love, Auntie.

writual

The call: I refuse to be reduced to the view _____
(word denoting persons who have harmed you) have of me. I
release myself of the burden of _____ (name
something you've been carrying because of that harm), and I
reconcile that who I was is no longer who I am.

The response: I/we stand in agreement with the truth that we
are all fearfully and wonderfully made. I/we value the fullness
and uniqueness of your lived experiences and affirm that all
of who you are matters to God. I/we support the healing journey you are on, as we offer our tears of joy for the saving work
God is doing in your life and tears of sorrow for all that you
have suffered as well.

Porch Talk

"I Found God in Me" and Other Lessons from Redemptive Self-Love

BEFORE WE DIVE IN HEADLONG and start rehashing and unpacking, Auntie wants to sit on this porch awhile and just be. Will you sit with me for a few and join me in the stillness?

. . . take a deep breath in.

. . . listen to your body.

. . . pay attention to what you notice.

Clenched jaw? Tight shoulders? Furrowed brow?

. . . let a long breath out.

. . . stretch your limbs and shake out your hands.

. . . roll your neck slowly.

. . . whisper aloud, "I am safe here."

Now, don't you feel better? I know I do. There's nothing like sitting still and having a good cry sometimes. Tears, regardless of what kind, are our friends and most fearsome advocates—if we allow them to be.

Let's review Auntie porch protocol. You know by now, we're gonna start with all the Tea first, then we will get into the honest-to-goodness Truth(s) because this set of letters was both heavy and full of heart. Here's the tea:

- Sugas: Those who are both fragile and flamboyant, awkward and awesome (aka neurodivergents) make our lives sweeter and so much more enjoyable while constantly navigating less than sweet circumstances and downright meanness from a world that does not value sensitivity.

- Niblings: Those who are transgender, nonbinary, or gender-fluid are a beautiful representation of the fullness of God—who (in the Christian faith) is God in three Persons—and cannot be contained by human constructions that limit their divinity.

- Love-makers: Those, typically women, who are stereotyped as promiscuous but are truly just self-possessed know far more about honoring their bodies than we give them credit for—simply because we have demonized pleasure and women's bodies. But desire is a gift given to us by God.

- Brave and brazens: Those who break generational curses and toxic relationships are often isolated from their families of origin because they disrupt the comforts of people stuck in disembodied practice and perpetual pain.

The truth about these groups of people is simple: they need, and deserve, tenderness. Yet, so often, they are tested and tried with little regard to how such interpersonal wrinkles and rips cause deep(er) wounds.

I begin with the necessity of tenderness because, from the well of my own lived experience, self-grace and self-love are commodities that it took a long time for me to understand and develop. And I believe that my sugas, niblings, love-makers, and brave and brazens likely all had to cultivate this very tenderness within themselves when no one else had any to offer.

The womanist tenet of redemptive self-love is to "esteem and reclaim the unique aesthetic aspects of Black femininity that normative society usually disparages."[1] It focuses on the necessity of self-love and self-care as acts of resistance and survival for Black women. Redemptive self-love involves affirming one's worth and dignity in the face of societal devaluation and oppression. It is about reclaiming a positive self-identity and recognizing oneself as worthy of love, respect, and justice. This tenet is a response to the internalized negative messages that Black women often encounter. What this means practically, particularly for Black women, is having the wherewithal and inner fortitude to pull ourselves away from death-dealing beliefs and internalizations to prioritize praising ourselves for the characteristics that society normally disparages on our behalf. In doing so, we not only defy what is out to kill us but also love ourselves fully and wholly. And loving ourselves saves us every time.

I translate the concept of redemptive self-love into the theological commitment of *tears as salvific work* because it is important we take seriously our own participation in that which can save us. Understanding tears as salvific work is to lay hold of the vulnerability that liberates us from all forms of self-harm and deprecation and invites us to the deep healing work necessitated by disrupting pain, silence, and trauma. It is the ability to allow weeping and other forms of lament to usher us into a radical acceptance of self. For many of us, this acceptance of self comes after denial and rejection from the very places where we should experience God's grace and love.

I recently watched a clip of an increasingly popular Christian influencer and social media televangelist speaking about gay people. The Auntie (short) version is that this woman believes that people can have same-gender attraction and still pray to God to renew their heart enough to not act on those attractions. As the clip made its rounds on social media, a colleague in ministry commented, "What in the [world] is she talking about?" (Auntie is being nice because y'all know my colleague ain't said "world.") And while I know my colleague meant the question rhetorically, I feel led to honestly contend with the inquiry. Because, indeed, what this Christian influencer described in her statement is an actual hell that she wants all Christ followers to live in as an expression of their faithfulness. I found myself wondering in response: What is it you believe about God—that God would want us to live a life filled with such suffering and self-denial so that we could somehow be "renewed"? What is it that you think hell really is, and why should so many have to experience a living version of hell right now, here on earth, simply because of whom they love?

I had a heart-to-heart with one of my dearest line sisters (a college friend who pledged the same sorority with me twenty years ago) about the influencer and her message. "I can't understand where the love for people was in her message," my friend said. "Was she suggesting that we should pray for people to be healed or changed out of love for them?" In the simplicity of her question, the most basic and fundamental answer revealed itself. No, we cannot proclaim to love God's people well when we hate ourselves or hate the very core of who people are.

In both the gospels of Mark and Matthew, Jesus is recorded as saying that the greatest commandment is to love God with all our heart and that the second is like it: to love our neighbor as ourselves. I guess in all my churchgoing and singing "Jesus Loves Me," I have come to prioritize the life and sayings of Christ in my own spiritual journey. So when Jesus instructed us to both love God and love others as ourselves, I understood that to mean that by loving others (well), we love God. And vice versa. This is why the "love the sinner, hate the sin" rhetoric that has become all the rage in our contemporary religious spheres is quite the conundrum for me, my friends. I cannot subscribe to "hating the sin" if that would require me to accept that the love between two consenting adults is something hateworthy—not when I know that God is love.

In a 2017 *USA Today* article, journalist Jonathan Merritt digs a bit deeper into the origins of "love the sinner, hate the sin." He reports that an early use of the phrase appears in Mahatma Gandhi's 1929 autobiography: "Hate the sin and not the sinner." But, writes Merritt,

> Gandhi's full statement has a bit different flavor: "Hate the sin and not the sinner is a precept which, though easy enough to understand, is rarely practiced, and that is why the poison of hatred spreads in the world." Gandhi rightly observed that it is difficult—perhaps impossible—to see someone else firstly as a "sinner" and to focus on "hating their sin" without developing some level of disdain for the person. Perhaps this is why Jesus did not ask us to love "sinners" but to love "neighbors" and "enemies."[2]

In Auntie's humble opinion, my guy Jonathan is onto something here. I cannot speak to that Christian influencer's life or relationship with God. But I can ask how she has presented God, the love of Christ, and her past experiences. She has openly admitted to still having same-gender attraction but has surrendered herself to God and is living in what she says is a happy marriage to a man with whom she now has children. And if she likes it, I love it. Yet, I still wonder: If she had gone a different way and allowed herself to be herself fully, would her message still be the same? And can you really love God's people if you do not also love yourself—fully as yourself?

We started this porch talk by taking a moment to gather ourselves. To breathe. To remind our bodies that we are safe. But I wouldn't be Auntie if I didn't keep it all the way real with you. Here's part two of the piping hot tea: Too many people—their bodies and their belief in who God created them to be—are not safe. Not within the four walls of the church. Not browsing social media. Not in and among their family members. And sometimes not even when they are alone with themselves and their own thoughts. Too often, this lack of safety—whether physical, emotional, spiritual, or otherwise—is created and maintained in spaces and institutions that are Christian. And this is why I intend to spend the rest of this time on the porch really considering the transformative power of tears as salvific work—especially when, historically, tears have been used as weapons by the oppressor and seen as a sign of weakness on behalf of the oppressed.

Let's do a closer reading of the Woman Who Loved Much text in Luke 7. Jesus is invited to eat at one of the Pharisee's houses. As they prepare to dine, Jesus is greeted by a woman whose name we do not know. We only know that she has a reputation as a "sinner." She stands behind Jesus and weeps—and then bathes His feet in her tears, drying them with her hair, kissing them, and finally, anointing them with ointment. We must not understate how vulnerable and raw this action would have been. Jesus' feet were likely covered in mud and waste from animals and other humans (is it not also wild that

Jesus' dirty feet were the gateway to her healing?). After telling a short parable to the Pharisee named Simon, Jesus tells him that the woman is forgiven—and because of the magnitude of her sin, that she, in turn, loves much.

What if this story isn't just about the "sinful" woman—who, by today's standards, would be viewed as a liability or a person not to consort with—but is also about how society viewed this woman as a problem and not a person worthy of being seen and loved? What if this woman's "sins" were not harms she inflicted on others; rather, what if they were indicative of others' feelings about her? We will never know the full story. We don't even know the identity of the Woman Who Loved Much. However, I know this much: as a woman who has been on the receiving end of others' narrow and damaging interpretations of who I am, I too have been forced to find Jesus in the most uncomfortable places. I imagine this woman would have preferred not to show up to a Pharisee's house just to get close to Jesus. But in desperation, she went into the home of someone who was perhaps complicit in her harm. All to get in touch with the source of her healing.

And what did she do when she got there? Did she—as I've been writing about through this entire book—speak up and tell the truth about her plight? No. Did she recruit her sista-friends and tribe to come with her? No. She did neither of these things. Instead, she did the only thing she could. She wept. And from her weeping, she cleaned the feet of Jesus and anointed them with ointment. Beloved, sometimes our weeping will lead us to "do the work our souls must have."[3] And sometimes the work our souls must have is the work of saving ourselves. From how society views us. From death-dealing circumstances. From what we believe about ourselves.

If the Woman Who Loved Much is anything like me, I struggled with that last bit a heck of a lot. I began to believe lies about myself and denigrated my self-worth because of all the things outsiders said about me. I'd never be pretty enough or girly enough or preacher enough or soft enough. I'd simply never be enough. Yet one day, something switched. After attending seminary and unlearning lots of horrible theologies and getting serious enough to regularly go to therapy, I'd had enough of not being enough. And I began to tell myself that I was enough. In the ever powerful words of Ntozake Shange that you've already encountered here, "I found God in [myself] and I loved her fiercely."[4]

Shange wrote *For Colored Girls Who Have Considered Suicide/When the Rainbow Is Enuf* in 1976 as a choreo-poem to tell the stories of seven women facing oppression in a racist and sexist society. (Shange coined the term for these poems choreographed to music and movement.) Many of the poetic monologues speak to the complexities of Black womanhood and include the full spectrum of our emotional experiences. And while Shange's work was both informative and instructive as I began to learn more about womanism, what strikes me most (even to this day) is the soul-baring invitation of her vulnerability. It was as if I could feel the moisture left by Shange's own tears on the very pages of my book as I read each woman's stories. And her tears—whether real or imagined—gave me permission to tend to the dry bones in my soul that needed a little watering to live and breathe again.

When I consider what tears as salvific work means practically, I think of the character T. T. from the blockbuster movie *Set It Off*. In the movie, a group of unlikely sister-friends (Cleo played by Queen Latifah, T. T. played by Kimberly

Elise, Frankie played by Vivica Fox, and Stony played by Jada Pinkett [Smith]) undertake an elaborate bank-robbing scheme in order to overcome years of disinvestment and economic disenfranchisement in the hopes that they would be able move their families out of the crime-ridden neighborhoods they've been stuck in. While Cleo, Frankie, and Stony are much more feisty and able to hold their own, T. T. embodies a child-like sensitivity and pure spirit that makes her the butt of many of their jokes. It also makes her susceptible to falling prey to how others see her. During the bank heist, T. T. gets scared and leaves before the raid is over. When the crew meets up after the heist, T. T. walks in apologetically and begins helping count the money. Frankie, seeing her as a weak link, decides that T. T. won't get her share of the money. But instead of accepting this judgment from Frankie, T. T. begins to cry. She demands that her crew see her. "I need this money," she says tearfully. Frankie finally takes off her tough exterior and apologizes, telling T. T. that she is her sister and handing her the money.

It may not seem revolutionary to y'all. But even in a dramatized format, T. T.'s tears forced those around her to see her as a human. A human who needed help and monetary support. Maybe if more people allowed their tears to escape from their eyes, perhaps we'd all be interrupted from our daily grind long enough to tend to those needing connection and support.

If you need a present-day, real-life example, Auntie has another on deck for you. Naomi Osaka is an emergent tennis champion who was blasted for her refusal to do press conferences during the US Open tournament. Citing her challenges with mental health, she broke down in tears after a tough 2021 loss to a teenage phenom and told reporters she would be taking an indefinite break from tennis. As outraged as fans and other people were at Naomi's statement, they had to stop and take notice of her vulnerability and humanity in that tear-filled moment. A moment which likely was the beginning of Naomi Osaka taking control of her destiny and saving herself from being devoured by the demands of competitive sports and impossible media outlets.

For all the people who have not been given room or the opportunity to see themselves for their own humanity and save themselves from the wiles of how society views them, I weep. I suspect that the Christian influencer I mentioned earlier may never have received such a transformative gift. To have that kind of safe space where you can be fully yourself and cry unashamedly is a sacred belonging.

I am not forgetting how much our society views or exploits tears in deeply problematic ways. Whether it's the tears of white women that, historically, have been weaponized as lightning rods for patriarchal values that protect them from "scary" Black men. Or the tears that Black children aren't allowed to cry because the world is never going to care enough to wipe them away. Tears are complicated. But what if we were brave enough to not let tears be used as weapons for division or characterized as weakness? What if we understood tears as, perhaps, the most intimate prayers we can pray with and for ourselves and one another? What if we reframed tears as part of the human rituals that will heal us rather than as reactions used to harm us?

As I learn what it means to parent a stubborn and smart and precocious toddler, I am relearning this (the hard way) every day. When I am at my wits end or my patience is at an all-time low with my daughter's tantrums, I often whisper to myself: "This is all she has." Angry and unreasonable two-year-old tantrum-ing tears are all she has when she does not yet have the spoken language to tell us what she needs. So I have to ask myself: Can she trust me to sit with her through her tears? To protect her from hurting herself until she is calm? To prod around in the dark and unintelligible until we figure out what we both need? These are the questions Auntie wants to leave y'all with, too. Because maybe you *aren't* the Woman Who Loved Much or the suga, the nibling, the love-maker, or the brave and brazen—who all likely need a shoulder to cry on. Perhaps your shoulders are the ones they need. Perhaps you are what I call a tear-sitter. Not unlike (but also a bit different from) a babysitter, maybe you are called to keep watch and comfort those who mourn. After all, Jesus said, "Blessed are those who mourn, for they will be comforted" (Matthew 5:4).

And maybe tears as salvific work is as much about the crier as it is about the community surrounding them. Because their tears might also invite us all to bear witness and become workers in the divine calling to help them get free. I hope you'll accept that invitation to be a trusted tear-sitter. I've outlined some tips just in case you think this is something God is asking you to do. It is not an exhaustive list, but it is a good start for those pursuing the theological commitments of sacred belonging.

Tip 1: Check out books that focus on tear-sitting and lament, like Henri Nouwen's book *Wounded Healer* or *Beloved* by Toni Morrison.

Tip 2: Unpack how you are wired to respond when someone cries in your presence. Do you feel the need to rescue them? Do you use scripture to rush them away from their pain? Try to get a sense for your own anxiety when dealing with people who are struggling.

Tip 3: Do some resource surfing (i.e., googling) to learn more about being a "non-anxious presence" with someone who needs support.

Last, but certainly not least—to all my sugas, niblings, love-makers, and brave and brazens out there, I see you. I pray that things get better. I pray that you will be able to let the tears flow and that you have plenty of tear-sitters to accompany you. And, most certainly, I pray that you will accept the role you play in salvific work. So that you may be healed. And completely free. Repeat after me:

I am free. . . No more chains holding me.

Praise the Lord, hallelujah, I'm free.[5]

—love, Auntie.

Transfiguration Is Social Healing

Jesus left that place and went away to the district of Tyre and Sidon. Just then a Canaanite woman from that region came out and started shouting, "Have mercy on me, Lord, Son of David; my daughter is tormented by a demon." But he did not answer her at all. And his disciples came and urged him, saying, "Send her away, for she keeps shouting after us." He answered, "I was sent only to the lost sheep of the house of Israel." But she came and knelt before him, saying, "Lord, help me." He answered, "It is not fair to take the children's food and throw it to the dogs." She said, "Yes, Lord, yet even the dogs eat the crumbs that fall from their masters' table." Then Jesus answered her, "Woman, great is your faith! Let it be done for you as you wish." And her daughter was healed from that moment.

—Matthew 15:21–28

If I didn't define myself for myself, I would be crunched into other people's fantasies for me and eaten alive.

—Audre Lorde, "Learning from the '60s"

THIRTEEN

To My Daughters and Deacons

(People Who Pretend to Be, or Actually Are, Churchy)

A PARABLE FOR MY DAUGHTERS AND DEACONS

When I think of "churchy" people, I sometimes have a visceral response. On the one hand, I can picture dozens of lovely elderly women who were absolutely the hands and feet of Christ. But then I think of the countless experiences I have had with "nice-nastiness" in church spaces and among the most "godly" of people. Over the years, I have found this dissonance to be very disconcerting, since most people of faith and preachers alike espouse a theology of welcome which says that the church is supposed to be a hospital for the sick and a safe haven for any and everyone. Meanwhile, a good number of us in the church struggle to live into the belief that we should be welcoming of all who enter. But let me say this right out of the gate: this is not going to be a cautionary tale of harms I've seen inflicted on other people. Nope. It would be much too easy to assume some sort of moral high ground by making this story about other people. I can't exempt myself from my own complicity with the behavior that I am attempting to examine here. Therefore, this story doesn't paint me in the best light. But it is necessary for me to share how easy it is for a daughter or deacon to become the very demon we pray against in our prayer closets.

Back when I was the youth director of my church (yes, the one where the pastor would eventually not affirm my call to ministry because of my gender), I handled every facet of youth programming—which meant that anytime an event was scheduled at the church for the adults, I would plan some concurrent activity for the young people. One evening, I'd come to church directly from my nine-to-five job, but Bible study wasn't set to start for another hour. I decided to sit out in my car and take a short nap. As I leaned back in my seat and closed my eyes, another car parked next to me. Two fellow church members got out of the car and began talking. I had the windows cracked and could hear everything they discussed—which, interestingly enough, was about me.

I guess they thought I was sleeping so they didn't use any filter with their commentary. The one women asked the other—who was a mother of some kids in the youth group— who was in the car sleeping. The mother answered, telling her who I was. She followed it with an emphatic "I can't stand that [woman]" (but with a much more explicit term). She explained that she had never liked me and how she hated that I was overseeing the youth ministry. The two women then turned to other church gossip as they continued standing right next to my car.

I still don't know why I did this, but I decided to get out and say something to the mother who had just given such poor remarks about me. Both of the women startled as soon as I opened my door. The first woman might have even said something to the effect of "Oh, we're sorry . . . we didn't mean to wake you." And I answered by telling them I wasn't asleep—and I had heard everything they'd said. Now, keep in mind that I was maybe about twenty-four or twenty-five and I was speaking to women who were ten or twenty years older. I was so nervous as I faced the mother who, apparently, couldn't stand me. I looked her in the eye and said, "I'm so sorry that you don't like the job that I'm doing with the youth and that you don't like me. I hope we can change that in the future." She was speechless, and I was shaking. I was so filled with anxiety and fear at how she'd respond that I believe it was a God-given reprieve that she didn't have anything to say. I left them there in the parking lot and went to find someone—anyone—who could give me a hug and some reassurance.

But, ah ah ah. Before you start thinking that's how the story ends, let me widen the angle so you see the picture more fully. Weeks before this incident in the parking lot, I'd done a reflective exercise with the kids during Bible study. At the end of each lesson, we would join the adults in the sanctuary and report out what the youth had learned. I don't remember what the actual activity was that particular evening or even the scripture, but it involved having the kids choose how they would handle certain made-up scenarios with their faith and trust in God. During our report-out, a brother and sister in my youth group—the children of the mother I encountered on the parking lot—shared with the group. They said something about how they had to learn to rely on God as a mother and father because their dad was in and out of their life and their mother had a lot of problems.

What I didn't know is that their mom, indeed, did have a lot of problems. Substance abuse. Chronic poverty. Lack of education. All things that made her relationship with her children extremely strained. Their mom, likely thinking I had purposely made her children report out and tell their personal business, had every reason to be embarrassed and angry at me. While I didn't knowingly mean for them to speak disparagingly about their mom in front of the congregation, it happened. And I'm not very proud of it. And I can understand why, weeks later, that lady likely wanted to cuss me out even more than what she said when she thought I was sleeping.

It probably seems like I'm telling that story to point out the mistreatment I experienced from a fellow church member. However, that explanation is far too neat, simple, and convenient for it to be useful for us. I share this particular parable to illuminate the many truths and multiple layers of reality that were present at the time. Within our church, we were always bumping up against damaging potholes in roads paved with our "godly" intentions. And rarely, if ever, did we talk about these disruptions and dissonances—even when they caused harm to our fellow church members. Rather than face the (sometimes) ugly truths with accountability, we resorted to over-spiritualizing and spiritually bypassing conflict.

Most of this behavior was influenced by what African American religious scholar Evelyn Brooks Higginbotham coined the "politics of respectability." Remember when I talked about Black families and child-rearing practices such as whuppings? That, unfortunately, is a result of respectability politics—the belief that behaving in a socially acceptable way would both uplift Black people and convince white people of our inherent value.

Higginbotham studied the politics of respectability in the context of the women's movement in the Black Baptist Church during the turn of the early twentieth century. She observed that engaging respectability empowered Black women to work against racist ideas and systems—but "their discursive contestation was not directed solely at white Americans," she writes. "The Black Baptist women condemned what they perceived to be negative practices and attitudes among their own people. Their assimilationist leanings led to . . . insistence upon Blacks' conformity to the dominant society's norms of manners and morals."[1]

Higginbotham names an interpersonal and identity-based phenomenon wherein politics of respectability "reform individual behavior and attitudes both as a goal in itself and as a strategy for reform." In other words, respectability politics encourages Black people to be respectable and shifts how white people see Black people as respect-worthy.

At my church, what this looked like, practically, was that there were all sorts of rules—spoken and unspoken—that we expected good churchgoing people to follow. And when people were not able to abide by those rules, regardless of the reason, we were meant to pray for them to get back into alignment with the expectations all while judging them for falling short. This became very prickly at our church because our membership included people from the Black middle to upper class as well as those who were struggling financially with limited access to resources and education that would provide upward mobility.

Of course, these struggles were not any fault of their own. Economic disenfranchisement and disinvestment was by design and is a byproduct of slavery and segregation. In our church, this meant that there were major class divides in the congregation itself that no one ever seemed to talk about head on. While I'd only ever known growing up in a household of stability and opportunity for education, that wasn't everyone's story in our church. Heck, it wasn't even everyone's story in my own family. But the real-life and material implications of such class divides weren't discussed from the pulpit. Therefore, when women showed up to church dressed what was deemed not appropriately or the man experiencing homelessness came in smelling like outdoors and alcohol, we looked down our noses at them rather than looking for the root cause of why they were struggling. As Higginbotham puts it, "The discourse of respectability disclosed class and status differentiation."

Perhaps the pastors I heard preaching in my youth and young adulthood found matters of class too political or too difficult to tackle. Yet we were always bumping into uncomfortable situations where class was the underlying issue without ever addressing it. The "nice-nasty" persona many well-meaning church folks projected was likely a symptom of these simmering tensions that we were ill-equipped to handle. I had no idea how to properly provide pastoral care or minister to teenagers whose parents were struggling with versions of life that I'd never lived. So I made mistakes when they came to me and expressed their feelings about their parents' personal lives. I was narrow-minded and judgmental and only knew how to read from the script of respectability politics that had been given to me. And if you didn't fit into those roles, I had no way to find connection or grace for you. My capácity to be a good gatekeeper for such perceived morality is precisely why that mother couldn't stand me. Because my perfectionism gave her little room to simply be a human who had pain points and needed the church's full support.

Hindsight is 20/20. And looking back, I thank God for the interior changes that have allowed me to both correct the course for the future and humbly offer wisdom for others. But as much as I have grown and cultivated a more expansive faith, much of that has to do with the Holy Spirit's transfiguring my view of Jesus. In the New Testament, the synoptic gospels describe Jesus taking Peter, James, and John up to a mountain to pray. There, Jesus is transfigured before them and light radiates off Him in glorious splendor. "The appearance of his face changed, and his clothes became as bright as a flash of lightning," says Luke 9:29. His disciples, who had been half asleep, finally become fully awake (talk about a stay woke moment) and realize who Jesus truly is. They'd been walking with Him for His entire ministry. And they still didn't know who He really was. The passages of scripture that describe this miracle outline my premise here: there comes a time in our faith that we must move from seeing Jesus as the friend who walks with us on our individual paths to salvation to encountering Jesus as a lover and liberator of all.

You see, the disciples had come to know Jesus as a familiar acquaintance. Yet the synoptic gospels (Matthew, Mark, and Luke) record that the disciples would one day see Jesus coming into who He was meant to be—the Son of Man who would set the captives free. All during Jesus' ministry of miracles and teachings, we can observe the disciples' lack of understanding of *who* they were with. They question Jesus' command, show signs of struggling belief or faith, and at times are unable to tap into the power Jesus was confident they had to help people in need. But that day on the mountain, I believe that all shifted for Peter, James, and John. Jesus was revealed not just as the guy they'd been galavanting all across Judea with. On that mountain, He was transfigured as the Son of God who would liberate us from all forms of sin.

This shift of seeing Jesus anew—not just as a personal savior but also as a prophet who was an enemy of the empire—means that we must also contend with how modern religion has attempted to depoliticize the work and witness of Christ. And in Auntie's case, this radical shift preceded a wonderful change that invited me to see transfiguration (of the Jesus I thought I knew) as social healing.

For sacred belonging, the theological commitment of *transfiguration as social healing* means we view sin as more than an internal, individual issue and accept that there are forms of sin that work collectively as evil and oppression against entire communities. It also means that we explore how internalized oppressions—like class divisions and anti-Blackness—show up in our churches and make daughters and deacons alike treat other people with blatant disrespect both interpersonally and institutionally. That disrespect may be treating a church member like you're better than them simply because you have more money in your bank account or discriminating against pastoral candidates simply because of their gender.[2]

The theological commitment to transfiguration as social healing requires us all to reevaluate how we live out our values as people of faith. Had I fully seen the transfigured Jesus, I believe I would have spied a bright light shining in the direction of my finding ways to connect with the mother who needed someone to see her beyond her faults. I would have been compelled to ask the deacons and trustees of the church to put systems in place where she could have what she needed (be it financial support or other resources). The transfigured Jesus would have taken me up onto a mountain on my "high horse" and awakened me from my ignorance and slumber. The transfigured Jesus would have flipped the tables of my creature comforts and asked me to get serious about advocating for collective healing in my community.

Well, just like I wasn't really asleep when I heard that mother say the quiet part about me out loud, I'm fully awake and woke enough to stand in the gap for those of us who are slower to hear the alarm clocks in our spirits. I hope to God that we are listening and ready for how we see Jesus to change. Imagine just how glorious our neighborhoods would be if we did.

A PRAYER FOR MY DAUGHTERS AND DEACONS

God who transforms our spiritual vision,
we thank You for not leaving us to our own devices when we are looking to move from faith to faith.
Forgive us, oh God, for allowing outdated scripts—inked by oppressive forces—to outline our thoughts and actions toward others.
Help us to be open to finding inclusive ways to be the hands and feet of Christ—
with renewed hearts that are not haughty while pretending to be holy.

Grant us the power to rebuke and strike down internalized oppression and external evil that seek to devour
and divide us from the inside out.

And give us grace and wisdom to know how to support
one another on our nice days and our nasty days and
everything in between.

May our vision now, and forever, be made right
with You—that we may see each other as sacred
belongings.

Amen and ashé.

A PROMPT FOR MY DAUGHTERS AND DEACONS

welcome

- Have you experienced "nice-nasty" behavior at the hands
  of churchgoers? How did you make sense of their treatment of certain people or issues?

- How does shifting your view of Jesus as a personal (i.e.,
  individual) savior to a prophet who was a threat to empire change your perspective of what salvation includes?

- How have you learned what it means to tear down
  strongholds and war against principalities? How might
  your faith be stretched to view them as calls to community and collective action?

witness

I have seen how churchiness has come into collusion
with respectability politics.

And how impossible rules infiltrate our faith spaces
and cause you to numb yourself to harm you've
experienced.

I've watched how you've tried to play nice when everyone
    else gets to be nasty toward you.

And I'm sorry that your pain was not met with grace and
    care.

I hope you know that churches are not meant to harbor
    hatred or harm.

And that you deserve to experience a Jesus that cannot
    be reduced to *kumbaya* messages with no power in
    His ministry.

For you are worthy of a transfigured Jesus that shines a
    light into all darkness—

and wakes us from our comfortable slumbers.

—love, Auntie.

writual

The call: I recognize the shortsightedness of seeing salvation as an individual _____ (word meaning path or
journey), and that this belief is _____ (phrase
meaning rooted or derived) in Western understandings of
individual thriving over and against the well-being of my
_____ (phrase meaning neighbors). I open myself
to the transfiguration of Christ in my life so that I may
_____ (personalized interpretation of Micah
6:8—do justice, love mercy, and walk humbly with God.).

The response: I/we stand in agreement with the truth that it
is our duty to fight for our freedom, our liberation, and our
collective wholeness. I/we embrace my/our part in wrestling
for the healing of ourselves, our neighbors, our kin, and our
community. And we will not rest until it is so.

FOURTEEN

To My Nieces

(All *Girls and Women*)

A PARABLE FOR MY NIECES

I have lots of nieces. Between my sibling's and sister-friends' children, I am always thinking about the next generation of Black girls who will one day be Black women who are running institutions, businesses, and families. My number one hope for them is that they will be unapologetic in who they are. That they will be big on purpose. And that they will not worry about taking up less space, because they are too focused on being who they want to be. My hopes for them are urgent and nonnegotiable—born from my desire for them (and all of you) to never have to experience learning how to shrink yourselves as I did.

When I was a little girl, someone in my dad's life did a lot of damage to my self-esteem. She never harmed me physically, but she did not treat me well and said negative things about me while I was in her presence. Her commentary about how I looked or the texture of my hair planted seeds of dislike for myself into my psyche. And it's taken me lots of intentional healing in therapy to uncover and work on those wounds. I wrote some of this healing into a poem entitled "Black girl magic":

> i learned how to vanish
> into thin air
> when i was little
> a witch taught me—
> made me do it
> because she couldn't stand
> the sight of me . . .
> so, i excused myself
> from taking up space
> in her lair.
> kept myself safe
> by becoming unmentionable
> because my silence
> always worked
> like a charm.[1]

Learning to shrink myself started there, in my dad's home when I was about five or six. But it didn't end there. From teachers who had no patience for me. To family members who lost sight of who I truly was. The messages I received early in my girlhood and on into my adolescence clearly communicated a necessary posture of acquiescence from me. I'm pretty sure that absorbing this message to shrink myself down is when I also developed the habit of slouching my neck. I've always been taller than most people and, likely in an effort to draw less attention to myself, I began bowing myself down unconsciously. Even to this day, I have to remind myself to sit up or stand up straight and hold my head up like the boss that I know I am.

It still scares me, though. Damaging messages get remixed and repackaged, sent to all the nieces in our midst who are unaware of how much those messages will cost them. So I want to talk about the internalized dimension of social healing. We have already talked about how transfiguration as social healing can shift how we see Jesus and thereby change how we show up for one another. Yet transfiguration changes our perspective not only of Jesus but also ourselves. Because when we commit to tearing down the strongholds of oppression in our own communities, that also requires us to tear down those strongholds as they show up in our thoughts about ourselves.

In Matthew 15:21–28, we meet a woman whom we know only as a Canaanite. In Reverend Auntie's theological imagination, I like to call her the Woman Who Warred for Her Daughter because she truly was put to the test as she asked Jesus to heal her ailing child. You see, as Jesus is out ministering and teaching, He encounters this woman, who begins begging Him to cast a demon out of her daughter. But there is just one tiny problem. Given the history and context of the relationship between Jews and the people of Canaan (located in present-day Syria), everyone knew that Canaanites were outsiders—misfits, if you will. The Greco-Romans considered Canaanites beneath them, and the Jewish people living under Roman occupation still considered Canaanites sorta-kinda like distant cousins that they could not get along with in any way. And because Canaanites were not the "chosen" people like the Jews and were not completely welcome by the Greco-Romans either, they had to navigate the world ever aware of who they were in others' eyes and mindful of certain boundaries they were not to transgress.

As the woman from Canaan approaches Jesus and asks for her daughter to be healed, she understands full well that she is a misfit. It would have been easy for her to acquiesce to the spoken and unspoken rules that would require her to shrink or fall back. However, she does not allow the past or problematic ideologies about Israelite-Canaanite relations to dictate her behavior. Despite the reputation of the Canaanites being sinful, pagan people, the woman does not let those negative stereotypes stop her from proclaiming that which she believes. She believes that Jesus is the descendant of the true King of Israel, and she lets the fullness of her belief in who Jesus is permit her access to the care she needs. She allows her belief in Jesus' power to overcome the boundaries of identity that have been placed on her. Because even though the structures of power have pushed the Canaanite woman to the margins of what is *socially acceptable*, she does not retreat to the fringes of what is *spiritually accessible*.

Matthew records an intriguing and uncomfortable exchange between the woman and Jesus. Not only does Jesus tell her that He has been sent for the lost sheep of Israel, He also tells her it is not fair to take children's food and throw it to the dogs. I cannot judge Jesus' intent with His response, so I am unclear as to whether He meant it to be derogatory (but let somebody call me a dog and see what happens). From what I gather, Jesus was not necessarily trying to be exclusionary, but He was well aware of the complicated history of Canaan, the power of the Roman Empire, and of His own

Jewish descent. Just as the woman was navigating the boundaries of her ethnicity in a Roman society, Jesus, too, was navigating the boundaries of His humanity amid His divinity.

Yet this woman, who is solely committed to warring for her daughter's healing, does not respond in anger. Rather, she repurposes the snide remark and says: "Yet even the dogs eat the crumbs that fall from their master's table." She subverts the demeaning insult into a divine interaction. In other words, she uses what Jesus called her to call God's hand. She uses what could have wounded her to do the work for her. This is the internalized dimension of transfiguration as social healing that I want all my nieces to understand. There are times when we must transfigure our relationship with Jesus and with ourselves. Because truth be told, there was a time in my life when if I'd experienced such pushback from Jesus, I would have absorbed it as having something to do with my own unworthiness. Yet the Woman Who Warred for Her Daughter shows us how to war for the wounded little girls within all of us. And gives us the courage to confront oppression even when it's housed within the holiest places.

What if the Woman Who Warred for Her Daughter had accepted Jesus' remarks as her portion? What if the world's or other people's definition of her was all she believed about herself? What if she never belonged to herself enough to speak up for what she wanted? These are necessary questions—especially when so much of our religious rhetoric and theologies are soaked with language of belonging to, and being used by, God. On the surface, I can relate to the comfort found in a sense of belonging to God. Heck, some of my all-time favorite gospel songs ("Lord, I'm Available to You" by Rev. Milton Brunson and the Thompson Community Singers and "I Give

Myself Away" by William McDowell) allude to this notion of belonging to God in the title. But sometimes, being God's possession can seem cringey and problematic. When I've spent time unpacking my religious upbringing and talking to other women who have had to reconcile their faith with who they were becoming, a common theme is the expectation that we offer our bodies as living sacrifices for God's purposes before we ever get the chance to define ourselves for ourselves. The result is that we find ourselves struggling with parts of our identity that do not seem aligned with what we've been taught is acceptable by God.

An example of this is the countless women I've spoken to who have struggled to enjoy sex and intimacy with their partner—even in marriage, which is supposed to be every woman's goal. They had spent years striving for a virginal aesthetic that required their bodies to be reserved for God and not for pleasure. So much so that when they actually got married, they found themselves uncomfortable when it came to sex and knowing their own likes and dislikes. They'd compartmentalized their sexuality for so long and labeled it as belonging to God that they never got the chance to learn it as something that was theirs to experience. This is why Auntie must reiterate the nuance found in sacred belonging. Because it is not just about feeling welcome in churches or other faith spaces. Sacred belonging is about trusting that God can handle the entirety of you and that you can too. Because there is nothing inherently holy about disavowing yourself of your agency and autonomy in service of God. In fact, I'm hopeful that in the time we've been spending together—between parables, prayers, and porch talks—you are coming to understand that you can both belong to yourself and deeply value God's authority in your life.

Multiple things can be true at the same time. And one of my Black feminist scholar faves Audre Lorde already gave us a prophetic word that captures what it means to be committed to transfiguration as social healing: "If I didn't define myself for myself, I would be crunched into other people's fantasies for me and eaten alive."[2] To all my nieces out there, understand that you are a sacred belonging to God, to your Auntie, but most of all, to yourself. Because as much as God gets the glory for creating you, you also get the green light to shape the kind of life you want to live, how you want to show up in the world, and who you wish to become. Above all, I hope that you will know how to stand in your truth before you shrink yourself for a lie. Because defining yourself, for yourself, is also your "reasonable act of worship/service" (see Romans 12:1) in a world that is preying on your downfall and hoping you believe in their fantasies of who you are supposed to be.

A PRAYER FOR MY NIECES

God who teaches us to boldly pursue our healing,
We thank You for agency and autonomy to define our-
    selves before the world determines who we are.
Help us, oh God, to be careful and cunning so that the
    wiles of oppression do not coerce us into forgetting
    our voice or our strength.
Forgive us for the times we've allowed other people's
    beliefs about who or what we should be to damage
    what You have already called good.
Give us wisdom to know how to be a sacred belonging
    as we walk in power and authority in our day-to-day
    lives.
Amen and ashé.

A PROMPT FOR MY NIECES

welcome

- When have you allowed other people's ideas for who you are supposed to be to affect the choices you are making for your own life?

- How can taking ownership over your autonomy (or inviting a niece in your life to take ownership of her autonomy) shift your relationship with Jesus?

- What are the beliefs, strongholds, or oppressive ideologies that continue to impede progress for girls and women (women meaning all women)? How can you begin to examine how those beliefs show up in your own life?

witness

I have seen how you are told to tone it down or turn
      down the volume.
And I know you sometimes struggle to feel comfortable
      with the sound of your own voice.
I want you to know that you are not the problem—
rather, you—in your fullness—are the solution.
Never give in to the weight the world tries to foist upon
      your shoulders.
Instead, walk with your head held high and, in the sky,
      where it belongs.
For you have been given a spirit of power and sound
      mind.
May they ever be your portion.

                                        —love, Auntie.

writual

The call: I recognize that there are some places in my own life where I have put _____ (phrase meaning limitations) on who Jesus is. And because of that I have also _____ (word meaning believed or absorbed) messages about myself that are incomplete or untrue. Today, I cast out the demons of _____ (list things you struggle with like doubt, low self-esteem, etc.) because I know I am worth so much more.

The response: I/we stand in agreement with the truth that it is our duty to fight for our freedom, our liberation, and our collective wholeness. I/we embrace my/our part in warring for the healing of ourselves, our neighbors, our kin, and our community. And we will not rest until it is so.

FIFTEEN

To My Loud Cologne-Wearers

(People Who Are Recovering Misogynists)

A PARABLE FOR MY LOUD COLOGNE-WEARERS

For a whole host of reasons, I've dreaded writing this letter. In the remixed words of beloved Maya Angelou, *and still I sigh*. Dread is likely not the best way to describe why this letter is hard, but considering how many loving family members and friends we all have who are (recovering) misogynists, I need to be forthcoming about how much care and caution I am exercising in this chapter. Whether you can identify them easily or whether you suspect there are some hints of disdain for women, you've likely smelled the strong aroma that typically radiates from this special group of people.

Picture it with me, if you will. You're at a family reunion or some other family gathering, and in walks your "uncle." He's in his mid- to late fifties, he wears socks with leather sandals and a Kangol cap cocked to the side or turned to the back. He is as loud as his cologne smells, and he always has the most to say on stuff he knows absolutely nothing about. He has conspiracy theorist tendencies and always has a pack of smokes and neatly folded dollar bills in his gold wallet clip. He is the "uncle" no one really wants to hug, but they do it anyway so as not to hear his mouth.

These "uncles" come in all shapes and sizes and ages. Even more concerning, many of their deeply held beliefs about women have been passed down to unassuming younger boys and men (and, yes, women and people of every gender too), who despite often having the privilege of being college educated and exposed to numerous opportunities, begin to uphold and espouse archaic views and values concerning women. And truth be told, its age-old ashiness. It's killing us—figuratively and literally.

I won't belabor the story by getting into too much triggering and traumatic detail—though I will warn you, this story talks about sexual assault. I knew a young woman in college who had an experience with a few upperclassmen that still haunts her to this day. These guys had a practice of inviting first- and second-year college students to their off-campus apartment to play drinking games with them. Once the young women became inebriated, the guys would take them into empty bedrooms where there was supposedly more "space" or more "drinks" to enjoy. My friend tells me she doesn't remember most of what happened that night, but that she knows she was too drunk to give consent. In the aftermath of what had just happened, my friend began to panic and asked her dormmate to take her home. One of the guys, who was majoring in law, used his best speech-giving and persuasion skills to talk my friend into calming down and staying. He told her that misunderstandings like this happen all the time and that it was not a good idea to get too hasty or upset.

When my friend later told me about what happened, she recollected how it felt like the guy who talked her out of leaving was insinuating that she should not tell anyone what had happened to her—not campus police, not her resident advisor, not even her friends. She felt that she needed to keep silent about what happened because she didn't want any investigations or interrogations of the young men who had invited them over and given underage young women alcohol.

While my friend's experience is horrible in and of itself, that's not where the story ends. Those upperclassmen responsible for assaulting my friend went on to be family men with great jobs and what appear to be wonderful lives. The one who talked my friend into staying went on to be a public thought leader for conservative Christian values. I cringe whenever I see his messages and posts plastered across social media. Because most of them reinforce ideals rooted in white supremacist, patriarchal standards—and without the proper critical engagement, people become willing carriers of messages that are meant to keep us bound.

I feel a holy rage when I think about how men with less than stellar sexual ethics become the poster-boys for silencing women. All while using the Bible to justify their stances regarding traditional gender roles and submission. Perhaps the most obvious place this is playing out is in the church, where many denominations still do not affirm women in ministry. Recently, in a landmark case, Rev. Dr. Eboni Marshall Turman filed a gender discrimination lawsuit against the historic Abyssinian Baptist Church for how they handled her pastoral candidacy.[1] Fellow clergyperson Rev. Calvin Taylor Skinner wrote an op-ed about it: "Learning to Walk Alongside a Leading Lady: Refining My Faith as a Recovering Misogynist." In his article, he acknowledges the errors of his ways and offers a corrective. "I now realize that love does not block," he writes.

> [Love] does not allow one's insecurities to be louder than one's will to change. Love does everything in its power to set its beloved free. In whatever role or capacity we share with our sisters, may love be the loudest. We cannot let sexism or misogyny hinder their capacity.[2]

Skinner names what I am attempting to unpack here. That being loud and wrong still makes you wrong. But being willing to be corrected by love will help you make it right.

Sexism and misogyny aren't just running rampant in the church either. It pops up on our jobs, in our homes, and sometimes (even for women) in how we see ourselves. I remember playing with my Barbie dolls as a young girl and creating whole story lines and characters where the women pandered for male attention and were the consummate damsel in distress. I laugh at it now, but it ain't no way I learned that from my momma. No, I learned to internalize misogynistic messages from TV, movies, and other members of my family. Whether it was dogging women for how they dressed or how many children they had, I became accustomed to women being a topic of critique and subjugation while men were allowed and encouraged to do whatever they wanted to do. Men having multiple children by several different women was acceptable. Men being liars, philanderers, and drug users was troublesome, but seemed to be normalized as acceptable too. Men being too "emotional" or having behavior thought to be too feminine—nope, they gotta go. Sexism and misogyny have so deeply infiltrated how we view women that we will even resort to hating men for being too much like a woman.

Misogyny is marked by extreme prejudice against or even hatred of or aversion to women. It aims to keep girls and women at a lower social status than men. It was misogyny (specifically, misogynoir*) that contributed to the departure of Dr. Claudine Gay from her post as president of Harvard University in early 2024. Dr. Claudine Gay served a short tenure after several leaders of Ivy League universities were asked to testify to Congress about school policies concerning antisemitism. This happened just as the ongoing Israeli-Palestinian conflict took a serious, catastrophic turn and the death toll was on the rise. Before the congressional hearing, a legal team advised several of the presidents who would appear. They gave very similar answers when asked about student conduct on their campuses. Dr. Gay was the only one to actively experience such a stark backlash. In the aftermath of people targeting her academic career, Dr. Gay made the choice to resign.

I encourage you to google her name. Click on any of the YouTube videos concerning her resignation and go straight to the comments. People laid the blame on thick. And unsurprisingly, they blamed Dr. Gay for plagiarism in her scholarly research—as notable Harvard alumni and media pundits scurried to report—rather than taking a step back to ask what else could be at play. Sure, the congressional hearing and the college presidents' testimonies were horrible. Yet people seemed to forget that each institution's legal counsel had advised those presidents how to answer questions about hate speech and actions on their campuses. And no matter how much apologizing Dr. Gay attempted to do directly thereafter, the vitriol only escalated. Even though the institution, including the board, rallied to stand behind her—the first Black president in its nearly four-hundred-year history—the attacks and plagiarism claims met their target. Critical engagement invites me to consider: in a time when a former US president is facing several cases of fraud, has been caught in lie after lie, and is *still* a popular candidate for the 2024 election cycle, is Dr. Gay's "plagiarism" what truly cost her the Harvard presidency? I have to laugh to keep from crying because I just know people are not serious.

Misogyny is more than just a few bad actors who hold narrow beliefs about women. It is an enterprise that creates and wreaks havoc on women and others in mundane and major ways. From the bedroom to the boardroom, no woman can escape the daggers it will throw. Whether it is controlling women's bodily autonomy or sexual or reproductive choices or subjecting women to horrible treatment and pay on their jobs, misogyny has a costly material impact on our well-being and livelihoods. More than just Dr. Gay have lost their positions because of it. The friend I shared about earlier suffered years of guilt and shame in the wake of her assault. I've also known women who left marriages, suffered severe depression, and struggled with self-betrayal simply because misogyny wrecked their home lives.

I am both relieved and thankful that people like Rev. Skinner have seen the light of transfiguration. Because without such an experience, he would still be a perpetrator of harmful patriarchy and misogyny that limits women's role in the church and the world at large. In his article, Rev. Skinner attributes much of his evolution to the Black women who had the patience and poise to walk with him through his ignorance and work with him until he could see the light of a new horizon. And he acknowledges that it should not have been their duty to labor alongside him until he got free of the oppression that bound him and, by extension, them.

I know we haven't made it back to the porch just yet, but I want to pause to invite all my recovering misogynists into some accountability and introspection with a few questions:

- Are the women and girls in your life safe with you? Not just physically safe. But also emotionally, spiritually, and mentally safe? Can they share the fullest range of their experiences and emotions without you jumping to silence *or* save them?

- Could you submit to, and be led by, a woman? On the job? At your church? In your own home? How would you serve under a woman's leadership? Would you do it gladly, or clenching your teeth?

- Have you considered what it means to be a woman and the daily terrors women navigate just to keep themselves from going insane or missing? How have you contributed to a woman's sense (or lack) of well-being?

- How often do you actually listen to women—especially Black women? How often do you ask women what they want you to know? And have you ever sat with a woman's critique of your actions so that you could actually respond thoughtfully and intentionally?

I suspect that if you, my beloved loud cologne-wearers, were to begin asking yourselves these questions, you also may experience a transfigurative experience like Rev. Skinner. Because the thing I've found in talking to my older brother or my husband or my father about my perspective, is that most times, they've never had to sit with the ugly realities of misogyny and their complicity in maintaining it.

I hope more recovering misogynists will begin speaking up and holding other men and unrepentant misogynists accountable for their behavior. I can't help but think about what might have happened if the pre-law guy had been my friend's ally and advocate rather than a salesman for remaining silent. There are way too many "good guys" who know the Miranda rights to misogyny by heart and recite them to vulnerable people who need them to disrupt its oppressive pattern rather than uphold it. If that upperclassman had stood up to his friends and called them on their deplorable behavior, my friend may never have been assaulted that night. But I guess that's why misogyny persists and is so pervasive. Because apparently collusion and cowardice are easier to handle than confrontation and courage when the "boys" get together and do what "boys" do. I pray I get to see the day when all misogynists have experienced transfiguration. Because when that day comes, we may all get to the social healing we need.

A PRAYER FOR MY LOUD COLOGNE-WEARERS

God who gives us second chances,

we thank You that You give us the opportunity to repent of our evil and ashy ways and be delivered from the chains which keep us bound.

Help us to see when we have allowed oppressive beliefs to become boundaries around Your radical love and care.

Forgive us for the ways we have participated in, and maintained, sexist, misogynistic, and patriarchal codes that have harmed girls and women in our midst.

And heal in us the places that those same oppressions have caused us innumerable harms.

For it is our reasonable act of service, to tear down the strongholds and principalities that keep us from treating one another as sacred belongings.

Amen and ashé.

A PROMPT FOR MY LOUD COLOGNE-WEARERS

welcome

- When and where did you learn that women are lesser than men? How was it communicated to you? How was it reinforced?

- How does Jesus respond to women in the New Testament? How does He treat and consort with them?

- Who are some women—whether in your life or leaders in professional fields—whom you can begin to listen to more? Create a list of podcasts, writers, and personal friends you want to start listening to.

witness

I have seen how locker room talk turns into language
that dishonors the women in your life.

And I see how little tiny attitudes and beliefs about
women can turn into machinations and fortresses of
evil.

I hope you know there's nothing manly about keeping a
woman down.

And that you will come to see the beauty in supporting,
seeing, and submitting to women.

For it is in listening to women that you will learn to love
them more fully and more freely.

—love, Auntie.

writual

The call: I recognize that I have a long way to go in how I
_____ (phrase meaning fix or unlearn) the
misogynistic ways I have engaged in for my entire life. And
I know that misogyny causes _____ (phrase/
example of harm) to the girls and women in my own life.
I want to do my part to dismantle _____
(name oppressions) that cause me and my loved ones harm
so that women are able to walk boldly in their truth.

The response: I/we stand in agreement with the truth that it
is our duty to fight for our freedom, our liberation, and our
collective wholeness. I/we embrace my/our part in warring
for the healing of ourselves, our neighbors, our kin, and our
community. And we will not rest until it is so.

SIXTEEN

To My Whippers and Snappers

(People Ranging from Gen Z to Millennials)

A PARABLE FOR MY WHIPPERS AND SNAPPERS

If you were alive anywhere during the nineties, then you've likely seen or heard of the popular blockbuster hit *The Problem Child*. The movie is about a little boy who gets adopted by a well-meaning married couple, who soon discover that their new son Junior is more than a handful. Junior causes trouble at school, in his neighborhood, and in his new home. His adoptive parents are at their wits end and want to send him back to the orphanage. But when they attempt to drop Junior off, they find out that he'd cycled through several families who had given up on him after they saw how challenging it was to raise him. Long story short: they end up keeping him and, despite their suffering a divorce and much more calamity in Junior's wake, Junior begins to settle into having a solid father-son relationship with his adoptive dad.

As I've progressed to the geriatric millennial phase of my life, my big age has allowed me time and experience and clarity regarding how and why people view younger folks, whom I lovingly call my whippers and snappers, as "problem children." Similar to how Junior left the orphanage and began wreaking havoc on his family's sensibilities, I truly believe that my generation and the generation behind me (Gen Z) have tap-danced on everybody's nerves. I suspect some of it has to do with growing up during the advent and emergence of digital technology, gaming platforms, and social media—which has legitimately changed humanity and how we do life. Yet I must also be honest that much of the flak we (and younger generations) receive feels more like unfounded resentment than corrective rebuke. If you read my letter to the seasoned saints, we've already covered some of this ground—I commonly hear people older than me say, "These kids today just don't . . . ". Fill in the blank with any negative attribution you can think of, and I've likely heard it in reference to my generation and those coming up behind us. These kids today don't want to work as hard as we did. These kids today don't know how to cope with real life. These kids today don't know how to talk to people. These kids today are soft. These kids today are, uh . . . kids, maybe?

Last I checked, our parents and grandparents used to be kids at one point too, right? Because when I hear these complaints, it sounds like folks are big mad but unable to think reflexively about their own lives and the evolution of society as a whole. What's more, if kids today don't know the proper way to conduct themselves, then isn't that a symptom of the systems of care responsible for them? Kids ain't just out here making themselves less than stellar human beings on their own. Kids are learning these behaviors from someone or somewhere. And kids are adapting to the times in which we live. I'm not sure what else we expected to happen when literal hell has broken loose in multiple ways during our and their lifetime. Natural disasters like Hurricane Katrina. The economic recession of the early 2000s. The attack on the World Trade Center. A debacle over the presidential election of 2004. Multiple wars, genocides, and mass shootings (at their schools, in churches, and other seemingly "safe" spaces). A global pandemic. An insurrection at our nation's capital after another debacle over the presidential election of 2020. All we (myself and other younger folks) know is the horrible reality of trying to believe in an American Dream our parents told us bedtime stories about only to be met with very daunting odds that any of those things could ever come true as we reach/ed adulthood.

We are not problem children. No, dear friends. We are simply problematizing what children shouldn't have to keep going through. It's why when I catch myself slipping into the "they are just lazy . . . they don't know hard work" rhetoric, I hurry to correct it with the question, "Why should we still be working ourselves to the bone?" Didn't my ancestors quite literally sacrifice their bodies so that we could see a promised land they'd never get to see themselves? Don't we get to enjoy the fruits of their labor? Goodness, it's like we are expected to view suffering as a generational inheritance. And I don't think that's healthy or necessary. Also, let's be clear. We have perfected the ethos of working smarter, not harder. So, yes. If there's an avenue to explore working remotely or taking more days off for mental health, that's a lane we're gonna take every time. That doesn't make us lazy. It makes us learners. People who learned from our parents and grandparents.

Watching *The Problem Child* now as an adult, I see multiple parallels for this intergenerational conversation. First of all, Junior was tired of the systems and institutions that discarded and recycled him rather than rendering him care. Likewise, whippers and snappers are tired of the systems and institutions that use them for free or low-paid labor and don't honor the fullness of our gifts. It's why so many of us are electing to go to brunch with friends and mimosas rather than coming to church on Sundays. Y'all know what I'm talking about. It is also why young people are not staying with jobs as long as our parents and grandparents did. If it's one thing whippers and snappers hate, it's being overworked and simultaneously undervalued. And as the phrase goes, when we can't "make it make sense," we will make our way somewhere else.

Also, like Junior, whippers and snappers are immensely clever. Chile, Junior gave all the adults in his life a run for their money. Not just because he was devious. But also because he was exceptionally smart and had a knack for being strategic. All he needed was the right mentorship and guidance and, dare I say, love. With that combination, Junior rose to the occasion and became a typical, thriving kid. I can speak from my own experience when I say that the people who have the most to say about millennials and Gen Z are the very people who cannot seem to be bothered to provide us mentorship and support. In turn, I know many of us have no semblance of healthy relationships with elders, nor have we been given the opportunity to build the stamina necessary to engage in tough conversations and respect "old school" discipline.

As I wrote to the seasoned saints, I still maintain that intergenerational cooperation is the necessary ingredient to addressing the underlying generational divides that are quite apparent these days. People in my parents' generation are indignant because whippers and snappers don't want to vote. Meanwhile, we are shaking our heads because our parents can't understand how we've become disillusioned with democracy (oh, hello, gerrymandering and voter suppression). And somehow, seeing one another as fully human with feelings and complex views and experiences gets lost in translation. Even more than these strained intergenerational relationships, I am concerned with what is at stake if we continue to allow polarization and division to keep us from the best parts of ourselves.

Ash-Lee Henderson is the co–executive director of the Highlander Research and Education Center, a social justice training school that has played an integral role in movements for labor and civil rights. Henderson is an amazing thought leader and activist for progressive organizing. In a recent post on social media, she discussed how conservative ideologues are gaining momentum, executing multi-tactical strategies, and garnering the support of masses of people who will support a policy playbook that will be detrimental to the health and well-being of millions of people. According to Henderson, the success of their strategy can be attributed to how they've navigated difference. Their strategy, she says, "speaks to regular people's fears and anxieties. It projects solutions, as they define them, and vision. It speaks to families, something folks can have faith and believe in, and belonging. It tells people what to do to throw down and how to do what's being asked of them."[1]

Henderson precisely calls out belonging as a necessary tool in bringing people together and building community and power. And while the aims of those conservative ideologues may be different from my own, I think their relational strategy could be the key to the intergenerational conflict we are experiencing.

Y'all, as sure as Southern sweet tea is thick with sugar, we have to be really honest about how movements for liberation have been stymied because we've disavowed our connections to one another. Because I figure white supremacy has long since understood that it will lose as long as there is a stable and solid connection between the elders and the whippers and snappers to come. What if seeing our elders as sacred belongings (and vice versa) is the very thing that would get us closer to conquering white supremacy and all forms of oppression once and for all? Who better then to give us wisdom on white supremacy's oldest tricks than the oldest members of our family? And who better then to usher us into a faster, more technologically advanced age of freedom fighting than us—the children born as digital natives?

Perhaps reconciling our differences with intergenerational dialogue seems silly or futile. But we have to consider that, even in its simplicity, it could be *the* transfiguration we need to get to some real social healing. Because it seems to me that when Big Momma 'nem was running those one-room schools and feeding the neighborhood and raising money for the church's ministries, more children had what they needed and flourished despite (and in the midst of) horrible white supremacist laws and leaders.

Sure, we can be truth-tellers and talk about the flaws and shortcomings of the ways of our forebears and elders. Because some of the dogmatics and tactics they used were overly harsh and entirely unnecessary. But I think remembering that our tribe is our sanctuary means we can also be honest about what wasn't working so that we can still work together to shape the world(s) we want to live in and give to *our* children one day. It is the idea of *on earth as it is in heaven* that Jesus taught us how to pray for in the New Testament. This is the beauty of the four-part framework of womanism and sacred belonging—all the tenets and theological commitments build on and inform one another. It will be the truth-telling that gets us back into proximity with one another (i.e., whippers and snappers with seasoned saints). It will be the tribe as sanctuary that troubles us to work through our differences so we can live alongside one another. It will be tears as salvific work that invite us to embrace and forgive ourselves and one another. And it will be transfiguration as social healing that requires us to get serious about believing that a modern-day miracle can happen right now if we are acting as the hands and feet of Christ. Because what if the story about Jesus feeding the multitudes wasn't just about hunger? What if it was really about a child in their youth who shows Jesus' disciples how to adjust their entire mindset about what is possible?

Maybe the Bible can fit many narratives and purposes. Some want (or need) it to be historically accurate. Others proclaim it as perfect and God-breathed. And still others know it as the closest thing we have to an incarnate God who lived and dwells among us. As for me, I understand the Bible as a collective sacred belonging that we must carry and hold on to and wrestle with together. Because doing so will mean we are committed to walking out our faith together—however messy and hard and beautiful and funny that turns out to be. I know it may sound overly optimistic. But in a world where a whole lot of things don't make a lot of sense, believing in one another sure makes a lot of sense to me.

To my fellow whippers and snappers, I believe in y'all. I believe in us. I also know we will be better off if we have the backing and support of our forebears. I know it's not easy nor lightwork to navigate the testy waters of harsh words and harmful behaviors. So I won't ask you to do anything that is not life-giving or affirming for your personhood. But I do encourage all of us to find two or three older people in our lives whom we are intentional about connecting with and learning from while we still have the chance. I'm just wild enough to believe that these small acts of love and kindness can turn the tide of power in our collective fight for freedom. I hope you believe it too.

A PRAYER FOR MY WHIPPERS AND SNAPPERS

God who honors our youth,
we thank You for allowing our exuberance to be a blessing and not a barrier to Your grace.
Help us, oh God, to be gracious with ourselves and those who came before us.
That we may learn to see each other—across our differences—as valuable and worthy of time and care.
Give us wisdom to see opportunities for collaboration rather than shying away from correction.
And offer patience and tenderness to those who struggle to see us and affirm us where we are right now.

For as we wrestle with how to show up with and for one
   another, we will learn to see each other as friends
   instead of enemies.
Amen and ashé.

A PROMPT FOR MY WHIPPERS AND SNAPPERS

welcome

- What are some of your fondest memories of spending
  time with your elders? How has your relationship with
  elders shifted over time as you've come into adulthood?

- What is it you want to say—with grace and love—to
  older generations? Make a list of both your grievances
  and gratitudes for them.

- What do you hope people remember about your generation—particularly, your strengths and greatest gifts?

witness

I have seen how your youthfulness has been weaponized
   and used against you—
all while being used for aims that are not your own.
And I notice how you struggle with the lack of respect and
   boundaries inflicted on you by those older than you.
Yet I hope you will find wisdom and mentorship with
   people who will push you and also be a safe space for
   you.
May you never give up on the sacred belongings, in the
   form of elders, that God has stored up for you.
For we will all be made better by the intergenerational
   bonds of love that lead us to new world(s) to come.

—love, Auntie.

writual

The call: I recognize that I am both powerful and capable while also being _____ and _____ (two different words meaning capable of being taught)—ever ready to learn from those who know things I may not know. I also acknowledge how _____ (phrase relating to age-ism or another form of oppression) operates to divide us and keep us separated from our loved ones. I am making a commitment to _____ (phrase meaning to honor) those in my life who are different ages and have different life experiences from me.

The response: I/we stand in agreement with the truth that it is our duty to fight for our freedom, our liberation, and our collective wholeness. I/we embrace my/our part in warring for the healing of ourselves, our neighbors, our kin, and our community. And we will not rest until it is so.

Porch Talk

"Make It Make Sense" and Other Lessons on Critical Engagement

IT'S GETTING LATE. I can hear the cicadas and crickets from where I'm sitting. The sun is setting just right, and it smells like rain is on the way. Honey, this is the perfect night to end our time together on this here porch. And it's been such a treasure and a pleasure, truly, to share my heart with yours.

Y'all know what time it is now, right? It's time for me to give y'all the final Tea first, then we will get into the honest-to-goodness Truth(s) after that. Here's the tea:

- Daughters and deacons: Those who pretend to be, or actually are, churchy are prone to rule-following based on fear and formulas—and people who are free from that disposition likely scare them even further into submission to said rules.

- Nieces: Those who are female have likely never been given permission to define, name, or own themselves for themselves before anything else . . . and that makes them susceptible to a life full of people pleasing and body bending that will ultimately cause them harm.

- Loud cologne-wearers: Those who are recovering misogynists need more spaces to unpack how misogyny has affected them *and* to hold one another accountable for nipping it in the bud when they see it.

- Whippers and snappers: Those ranging from Gen Z to millennials (and the generations to come) are going to up-end life as we know it—for the better. And I'm here for it.

And the truth of the matter is that every single one of the people in these groups deserve careful observation and a consistent offering of support. Yet we are often too polarized to pay attention to their unique needs. So instead we rely on reductionist narratives about them and base our relationships with them on these half-truths.

This is why I consider the theological commitment of *transfiguration as social healing* as both the most difficult and most rewarding element of sacred belonging. To be serious about this commitment, we must accept the communal aspect of our faith over and against a Westernized notion of individual salvation unconcerned with the well-being of others. It is the invitation *do justice, love mercy, and walk humbly with God* as a reasonable act of service in tearing down the strongholds of oppression (white supremacy, sexism, misogyny, homophobia, transphobia, xenophobia, Christian nationalism, ableism, etc.) as a form of spiritual warfare within us and in our communities. And, if I'm keeping it all the way real, you simply cannot commit to this practice without prizing critical engagement as a necessary tool for survival in an oppression-ridden world.

Critical engagement, the fourth tenet of womanism, tells us that Black women "possess the unique capability to transform society by imparting a liberating vision of a just and inclusive world."[1] Author Zora Neale Hurston once said that Black women are the mules of the earth. She meant that we are simultaneously disregarded and expected to bear the brunt of the labor that needs to be done. And because of this precarious position, Black women also have the solutions that will free us of the oppression that causes such harm. That is critical engagement. It calls for us to actively and analytically examine and challenge oppressive structures and ideologies that affect us. It involves critiquing both the broader social systems (such as racism, sexism, and classism) and the specific ways in which religious traditions have perpetuated these injustices. It undergirds the mantra "Listen to Black women." You, my friend, have already begun accepting this reality because you've nearly read an entire book by a Black woman in the hopes that something I have to offer will help liberate you in your own journey. But what would happen if, on a global scale, people began to really #BelieveBlackWomen? That is at the crux of critical engagement and transfiguration as social healing, the final theological commitment of sacred belonging.

The Oxford definition of *transfiguration* is "a complete change of form or appearance into a more beautiful or spiritual state." In biblical texts, as we've discussed, transfiguration is described in terms of Christ appearing in radiant glory to three of His disciples. On Auntie's porch, transfiguration is about allowing our beliefs about God, about Jesus, and about who we are to be radically transformed when necessary. Of course, this would mean that to #BelieveBlackWomen, we would inherently have to shift how we handle what society has told us about Black women. Similarly, it would also mean we would have to be okay with challenging how the church and our beloved faith leaders have shaped what we believe about God. I chuckle aloud at the thought. Because some of y'all, while unaware, are so bound up in orthodoxy and orthopraxy that you can't even begin to consider what trans-figuration would look like for you.

Allow me to explain. Orthodoxy is an emphasis on correct belief. And orthopraxy is an emphasis on correct conduct. In a practical sense, this shows up in our churches and faith spaces in how we perform certain rituals (baptism, commu-nion, etc.) and how we interpret certain practices and doc-trines (confession, repentance, sanctification, etc.). I suspect that many folks who describe themselves as Christian likely have overcommitted to orthodoxy and orthopraxy[2] and undercommitted to exploring the fullness of identity with and in Christ.

In this way, I fear most people remain so rigid in the struc-ture of their beliefs that transfiguration—a literal and total change in what they are used to seeing—would be nearly impossible. Such a sad waste of faith, in my humble opinion. Because what good is a faith that can't move you to believe something you ain't never seen before? What good is faith if you're not going to allow it to rock you to your core and shift your thinking every once and a while?

Honey, listen . . . there was once a time that if someone said I'd be friends with, and welcoming of, gay people—I'd have laughed in their face (a good, hearty laugh at that)! But along my journey, transfiguration took hold of me and changed me from the inside out and challenged me to see God in stretching and terrifying ways. And you know what? I am so glad about it. Immensely and eternally glad about it. We've talked about the Woman Who Warred for Her Daughter as a biblical example of transfiguration as social healing. This woman defied what was standard practice and belief—that is, orthopraxy and orthodoxy—and got indignant with Jesus

Himself to get healing for her daughter. What makes us think it is unreasonable or even unrighteous to flip over tables of oppression in our churches? And would facing temporary insult prevent us from getting closer to God?

So, dear friends, I want to ask you: What is it that you would get indignant with Jesus about? Who is important enough for you to risk everything to get healing for them? And what might be keeping you from believing in the fullness and expansiveness of God?

That's what is at stake when we do not understand critical engagement or practice transfiguration as social healing. We run the risk of injury—causing ourselves deep emotional, psychological, and spiritual harm—all in the name of (our beliefs about) God. I'll be the first to say, I don't want to believe in a God like that. You can have it because Auntie don't want it. And, to be clear, I don't think God needs or wants it either.

That's why I'm so glad folks like the whippers and snappers of the world are already showing us (better than they can tell us) what exploring the fullness of their identity with, and in, Christ. Take, for instance, young rapper and college basketball phenom Flau'jae Johnson. My honorary forever niece is currently a sophomore at Louisiana State University playing guard for the women's basketball team (which won the National Championship in 2023). While balancing her basketball and collegiate obligations, Flau'jae is also an up-and-coming rapper who first debuted on the reality television series *The Rap Game* in 2017. Little sis is breaking molds and being herself unapologetically as she excels as a scholar-athlete and burgeoning music mogul and business professional. Boasting several NIL deals and partnerships, she owns all the rights to her music and aspires to have her own music label.

I uplift young niece Flau'jae for a couple of reasons. First, like the Woman Who Warred for Her Daughter, Flau'jae refuses to be put in boxes assigned to her and is coming for everything God has stored up for her. In one of her most popular songs, "Big 4," she raps about how people constantly ask her to choose between ball and a music career. To which she responds in one of the lyrics, "I'm still doing both so why you asking me?"

Flau'jae's ability to do her—as in be completely herself—and supersede whatever barriers and boundaries people attempt to put on her is unparalleled. And it's a gift I wish I'd cultivated earlier in my life. What's more, Flau'jae represents a growing class of young people who are extremely socially conscious and feel responsible for making sure their communities are thriving. In numerous songs, she has rapped about unfair systems of economic disenfranchisement and racism that lock her community out of opportunity and safety. And any chance she gets, she goes to her hometown, Savannah, Georgia, and spends time with the youth and donates to local nonprofits that are the village-keepers of the community. I imagine Flau'jae understands both the internalized and outward expressions of social healing—that by defining herself as a rapper and a hooper before anyone else tried to stop her, self-determination allowed her to declare it her responsibility to make sure everybody back home was eating good. Her willingness to live fully into who God designed her to be also opened doors for her to do justice, love mercy, and walk humbly with God as a community servant concerned with the well-being of those around her. I'm not certain that

Flau'jae would be where she is if she didn't believe that God could handle the entirety of who she is. She consistently gives God credit for her successes thus far, and in my proudest Auntie way, I sincerely believe that God is pleased in who she is and everything that is to come for her.

I wouldn't be a good Auntie if I didn't follow up such a feel-good perspective with the not-so-pleasant implications of transfiguration as social healing. Because as amazing and popular as Flau'jae is, there are difficult aspects of what this theological commitment will mean or means for those of us who are figuring out what it looks like in the public discourse and in our faith practices. Earlier, we considered Dr. Claudine Gay's resignation from Harvard University. Understanding the multiple realities within what happened to Dr. Gay means that we will have to be honest about how intersectionality requires us to go deeper and be more honest. Dr. Kimberlé Crenshaw pushes us to reconsider what intersectionality means. It's not just about identity, she writes.

> It's about how structures make certain identities the con-
> sequence of, the vehicle for, vulnerability. . . . You've got
> to look at the context. What's happening? What kind of
> discrimination is going on? What are the policies and
> institutional structures that play a role in contributing to
> the exclusion of some people and not others?[3]

If we ask these questions, we must consider why Dr. Gay resigned the Harvard presidency against the backdrop of a genocidal conflict between Israel and Palestine. Because just as the Woman Who Warred for Her Daughter was un-chosen and seen as a problem because of her ethnicity, Dr. Gay was up against the same adversity. Just as the Simon the Pharisee chided Jesus for permitting the Woman Who Loved Much into the place where they were eating, there was a concerted and collective effort to question Dr. Gay's position as an authority of Harvard. And much of that effort was undergirded by religious rhetoric and affinities that most people don't want to be honest about.

Back in the mid-2010s when I was still super saved and a self-proclaimed holy roller, I joined an international Bible study group. It was really nice at first. To have community with other believers and commit to weekly study was exactly what my soul needed. But underneath the study time were strange (and deeply) problematic messages about God's providence and promises for the modern nation-state of Israel. The leader of the Bible study would stand in the pulpit and tell hundreds of good Christian people that nation after nation would have to bow down when God decided to bless Israel with the land God promised them—and that we, as Christians, should do everything in our power to be on the side of Israel when that happened. It was the Christianized translation of Zionism, a nationalist movement to establish a homeland for the Jewish people, particularly in Palestine.

Given the magnitude of the death toll in the ongoing Israel-Hamas war, I honestly shudder now just thinking about how I soaked up those Bible study messages with not one ounce of critical engagement. That I never considered how God's apparent allegiance to Israel alone could mean apartheid, brutal treatment, and mass death for Palestinians is downright frightening. This uncritical loyalty to dangerous theologies is causing so many Christians not to see the full picture of how so-called freedom for one group can end up creating oppression for another. And it angers me that so many people, in their haste to be supportive of the state of Israel, agreed that Dr. Gay should pay the price with a resignation.

My mind also goes deeper in time to other examples of the deep work and spaciousness we must create in order to be serious about transfiguration as social healing. Let's talk about the beloved character Claire Huxtable from *The Cosby Show*. For many of us (including Auntie), the actress who played Claire—Phylicia Rashad—is either the mother we wish we had or the honorary Auntie we pretend we know. On the show, she was brilliant, beautiful, and a boss on the job and in her home. We love(d) Claire because she made us proud to be Black. And because she belonged to us. Yet so many people were incensed when the actress—who is a whole entire human with a whole host of lived experiences—offered vocal support of her former costar Bill Cosby amid his legal troubles for sexual assault.

It is baffling to me that Phylicia Rashad would publicly applaud Bill Cosby's 2018 release from prison—but that's not my point. The point is that we have to learn how to make room for the fullness of who people once were, who they are now, and who they might become. I hate that the memory of our beloved Claire Huxtable has been besmirched by her proximity to or support of someone who inflicted great harm to countless women. But I can honor what she meant to us all (as the character Claire Huxtable) while also pointing out how deeply hurtful her actions likely were to the people who had been harmed. We don't have to be so stuck in binary thinking all the time. This is the chokehold I want us to stop signing up for, my friend. Because it's messing up the breaths we breathe and the lives we lead.

Come close while I whisper the quiet part out loud. In the words of the Big Homie, Jesus, in John 5:6, *Do you want to be made whole?* (NMB). And a necessary corollary: Do you want to be free, beloved? God knows I do. So, I choose transfiguration. Not just once. Not just twice. But as many times as it is required. Transfiguration as social healing gives us the range to consider how our most beloved can behave in horrible ways under the auspices of empire. Transfiguration as social healing helps us interrogate how we all play a part in the oppressions that ensnare us and how we can all play a part in getting us free from such entanglements. Transfiguration as social healing requires us to divest from such limiting and narrow interpretations of individual prosperity and to work toward building a world where everyone has what they need. That ain't socialism, my friend. That's Bible. When the early church was formed as recorded in Acts, we learn that all the believers worked in unity, sold all their possessions, and distributed the proceeds "as any had need" (Acts 4:35).

In my grandmother's house, as is custom in the homes of many Black seasoned saints, my grandmother kept a picture of Jesus handy near her Bible. I eventually realized that the iconic photo, which pictured Jesus as a sandy blonde-haired and blue-eyed man, was the all-time most-reproduced image of Jesus: *Head of Christ* by Warner Sallman, commissioned in 1940. I always thought it was strange that this mainstream image found its way into Black homes, but I didn't question my grandmother or her faith. But something interesting happened when I was a teenager. My grandmother received a newer, nicer, and larger photo of Jesus in a beautiful frame as a gift. Only this time, Jesus was a deep, chestnut brown-skinned man with long, black locs down His back. She placed the frame in the middle of her living room where everyone could see it. And this simple shift from the 1940s blonde-haired Jesus to the "I'm Black and I'm proud" Jesus staring back at me changed who I believed Jesus could be. It's not that I needed Jesus to be some racialized avatar who looked like Tyrone from up the block. Rather, opening myself to the layers of Christ's being and seeing Him transfigured before me gave me room to see the work of God and my own faith differently. And that's really the crux of what I'm asking you to do in your own faith walk, too. Let Jesus be fully Jesus—even if it's different from how you ever imagined Him—while you are fully you.

Perhaps this seems daunting. Or maybe you don't know where to start. That's okay. I don't think this process of engaging sacred belonging and the theological commitments must be a linear one. And I definitely do not want to prescribe rules and thereby undo all the work of helping you understand why such rigid rule-following will never get you to the freedom you seek. But I will offer that a good place to start is to take a spiritual self-inventory:

- What is your earliest or fondest memory of the church or your faith journey?

- Describe a moment where your lived experience was no longer congruent with your spiritual or faith formation.

- How did that moment affect your relationship with the church or your faith?

- How has your faith journey influenced how you see yourself?

- How has your faith journey influenced the way you see God or the church?

These questions might seem straightforward. Yet I think you'll find that they invite deep introspection that can help you explore the contours and disruptions of your faith journey. And, hopefully, they can also encourage you to cultivate the four theological commitments of sacred belonging: truth-telling is spiritual discernment, tribe is sanctuary, tears are salvific work, and transfiguration is social healing.

Now, it wouldn't be a proper porch talk if Auntie didn't leave you with a few tips to help you dig into that final commitment.

Tip 1: Make a list of the three most salient social ills that are apparent in your respective community. Align that list with nonprofit organizations, advocates, and faith-based activists who are working to eradicate those social ills. Select one issue and organization to support (tangibly with resources or donations) or volunteer with regularly.

Tip 2: Write a letter of agreement with yourself that explains why the issues you selected connect with your faith and your concern for the well-being of others. Be sure to use Jesus' ministry to support your claims.

Tip 3: Reread Dr. Kimberlé Crenshaw's questions about intersectionality. Answer those questions regarding the social ills or issues you outlined in tip #1. Please do thorough and accurate research to understand the layers of contributing factors.

Tip 4: Try to paint a picture of transfigured Jesus—either with a written description or a hand-drawn or digital sketch, if you are able. Describe what Jesus as both a lover and a liberator looks like, how He moves in the world, and who He embraces and offers healing to.

Now, go and do likewise.

—love, Auntie.

A Benediction for My Sacred Belongings

One of my favorite benedictions is Numbers 6:24–26:

> The LORD bless you and keep you;
> the LORD make his face to shine upon you and be gra-
> cious to you;
> the LORD lift up his countenance upon you and give you
> peace.

I've had to speak this blessing and benediction over myself many, many times while writing this book. I didn't know how deeply cathartic and hard and beautiful this process would be. It almost took me out and landed me on the other side of glory like a solid 2.5 times since I started (but that's a different story for a different day). Either way, beloved, you need to know that you were worth all of it. Especially if it means that you and your faith have been changed, challenged, comforted, or consoled. Listen, I know life has felt like a never-ending roller coaster careening from dumpster fire to pure bliss. And, yeah, quite a bit of what we've all been experiencing over the last few years is certainly zero stars, do not recommend.

But you, my dear one, are so worthy of believing there's more out there than sadness, sin, and suffering. And for that reason, I'm going to leave you with the same words we started with and ask that you say them to yourself aloud as a reminder of what you deserve:

My faith is a sacred belonging.
A gift that makes room for who I am becoming;
a gift that I do not own alone but welcomes my owner-
    ship of the co-journey.
I am worthy of experiencing sacred belonging.
A place where, when I am *still* enough, I hear God's voice
    saying: you are still *enough*.
Regardless of what has tried to kill me and has failed.[1]
We are a sacred belonging.
To a Creator who can handle all of who we are and who
    we are not.
May we find and create the sacred belonging.
That will heal us from the ills that try to make us believe
    we do not belong together.

Glossary (on Auntie's Terms)

Beloved community—A term frequently referenced by Rev. Dr. Martin Luther King Jr. and attributed to theologian Josiah Royce, beloved community represents an ideal society where all people live together in a spirit of cooperation, justice, and love. In this community, poverty, hunger, and homelessness are eradicated and discrimination, bigotry, and prejudice are replaced by an all-encompassing spirit of inclusiveness and mutual respect. Beloved community is not simply a utopian vision but a realistic, achievable goal that requires commitment, action, and systemic change to address and overcome social injustices.

Hermeneutic of suspicion—A critical approach to interpreting texts and social phenomena, initially discussed by philosopher Paul Ricoeur. This method involves questioning and scrutinizing the underlying assumptions, power structures, and hidden agendas within texts or social practices. It assumes that surface meanings may conceal deeper truths or ideologies that need to be uncovered and critically examined. Womanist theologians, building on the work of Alice Walker and others, have further utilized the hermeneutic of suspicion to analyze religious texts, traditions, and practices from the perspective of Black women's experiences. They use this approach to challenge interpretations that have historically marginalized or oppressed women, especially Black women. By applying a hermeneutic of suspicion, womanist theologians seek to uncover and address the ways in which sexism, racism, and other forms of injustice are perpetuated through religious and cultural narratives. This enables them to advocate for more inclusive and liberating interpretations that affirm the dignity and worth of all people, particularly those who have been marginalized.

Intersectionality—A concept developed by scholar Dr. Kimberlé Crenshaw as an analytical framework that examines how various aspects of a person's social and political identities—such as race, gender, class, sexuality, ability, and more—interact and intersect to shape their experiences of discrimination and privilege. Intersectionality highlights that these identity categories do not operate in isolation but rather interlock and influence one another, creating unique and multifaceted experiences for individuals. For example, the experiences of a Black woman are distinct from those of a white woman or a Black man because the overlapping identities of race and gender create a specific set of challenges and opportunities. Intersectionality aims to reveal and address these complex and often overlooked dimensions of inequality and social injustice.

Kin-dom versus kingdom—The shift from "kingdom" to "kin-dom" is an effort by some religious scholars to use language that better reflects the values of inclusivity, equality, and relationality in the community of God. It moves away from hierarchical and patriarchal connotations, promoting a vision of divine community based on mutual respect and kinship. It also gives people a way to use gender-neutral, decolonized language for theological discourse.

Misogyny and misogynoir—The general hatred, contempt, or prejudice against women. It encompasses a wide range of behaviors, attitudes, and institutional practices that devalue, belittle, or harm women simply because they are women. *Misogynoir*, a term coined by scholar Moya Bailey, addresses the unique forms of misogyny that affect Black women. It combines *misogyny* with the French word *noir*, meaning "black," to highlight the intersection of racism and sexism.

Sacred belonging—A dialogical and embodied space for faith exploration (from all walks of life) that invites the fullness of one's identity, spiritual expression, and theological beliefs in accordance with womanist, anti-oppressive values.

There are four theological commitments (as adapted from the tenets of womanism):

1. *Truth-telling is spiritual discernment*—To associate seeing and speaking truth (to power) as a necessary form of faith expression and Christian witness. It also affirms the vital nature of God-given agency to change or impact our surroundings—particularly, in instances of oppression and unfairness. Examples: Queen Esther (Esther 4), Angela Davis, Sister Mary Clarence (from *Sister Act*), Meghan Thee Stallion.

2. *Tribe is sanctuary*—To recognize that the intentionality with which we choose to build our chosen family or village of support oftentimes results in life-giving,

life-affirming relationships akin to divine places of safety. It is to live into the call to be(come) sources of refuge for one's self and others who otherwise would not experience care, inclusion, or welcome. Examples: Miriam (Exodus 2), Fannie Lou Hamer, Shug Avery (from *The Color Purple*), Lizzo.

3. *Tears are salvific work*—To lay hold of the vulnerability that liberates us from all forms of self-harm and deprecation and invites us to the process of deep healing work necessitated by disrupting pain, silence, and trauma. It is the ability to allow weeping and other forms of lament to usher one into a radical acceptance of self. Examples: the Woman Who Loved Much (Luke 7), Ntozake Shange, T. T. (from *Set It Off*), Naomi Osaka.

4. *Transfiguration is social healing*—To accept the communal aspect of our faith over and against a Westernized notion of individual salvation unconcerned with the well-being of others. It is the invitation *do justice, love mercy, and walk humbly with God* as a reasonable act of service in tearing down the strongholds of oppression (white supremacy, sexism, misogyny, homophobia, transphobia, xenophobia, Christian nationalism, ableism, etc.) as a form of spiritual warfare within ourselves and in our own community. Examples: the Woman Who Warred for Her Daughter (Matthew 15), Claudine Gay, Claire Huxtable (from *The Cosby Show*), Flau'jae Johnson.

Sex positivity—An attitude towards human sexuality that embraces and affirms sexual expression and consensual sexual activities as healthy and normal aspects of life. The sex positivity movement encourages open, honest, and respectful discussions about sex, sexuality, and relationships without shame or judgment and seeks to create a culture where individuals feel empowered to explore and express their sexuality in autonomous, fulfilling, and safe ways.

White supremacy—"The idea (ideology) that white people and the ideas, thoughts, beliefs, and actions of white people are superior to BIPOC communities and people and their ideas, thoughts, beliefs, and actions. While most people associate white supremacy with extremist groups like the Ku Klux Klan and the neo-Nazis, white supremacy is ever present in our institutional and cultural assumptions that assign value, morality, goodness, and humanity to the white group while casting Black, Indigenous, and People of Color as worthless (worth less), immoral, bad, and inhuman and 'undeserving.' Drawing from critical race theory, the term 'white supremacy' also refers to a political or socio-economic system where white people enjoy structural advantage and rights that other racial and ethnic groups do not, both at a collective and an individual level."[1]

Womanism/womanist—Terms coined by Alice Walker.

1. From *womanish*. (Opposite of "girlish," i.e. frivolous, irresponsible, not serious.) A Black feminist or feminist of color. . . . Usually referring to outrageous, audacious, courageous, or *willful* behavior. . . .

2. *Also*: A woman who loves other women, sexually and/ or non-sexually. Appreciates and prefers women's cul-

ture, women's emotional flexibility, . . . and women's strength. . . . Committed to survival and wholeness of entire people. . . .

3. Loves music. Loves dance. Loves the moon. *Loves* the Spirit. Loves love and food and roundness. Loves struggle. *Loves* the Folk. Loves herself. *Regardless.*

4. Womanist is to feminist as purple is to lavender.[2]

Womanist theology—"A religious conceptual framework which reconsiders and revises the traditions, practices, scriptures, and biblical interpretation with the specific purpose and lens to empower and liberate African/American women"[3] and others experiencing interlocking oppressions. According to scholar Emilie Townes, it is a necessary "reflection that places the religious and moral perspectives of Black women at the center of its method. Issues of class, gender (including sex, sexism, sexuality, and sexual exploitation), and race are seen as theological problems. Womanist theology takes old (traditional) religious language and symbols and gives them new (more diverse and complex) meaning."[4]

Four tenets of womanist theology, as defined by Rev. Dr. Stacey Floyd-Thomas[5]:

1. Radical subjectivity: The foundational moral principle that guides the liberation of Black women and dictates that Black women must assume a defiant posture and audacious, inquisitive nature in order to rise above their circumstances and experience that which otherwise would be denied.

2. Traditional communalism: The way in which the practical and common sense of Black women support the survival and success of the Black community.

3. Redemptive self-love: To esteem and reclaim the unique aesthetic aspects of Black femininity that normative society usually disparages.

4. Critical engagement: The assumption that Black women possess the unique capability to transform society by imparting a liberating vision of a just and inclusive world.

For all the little girls who needed to see.
For all the grown women who needed to know.
That belonging begins within.

Notes

Foreword

1 Imani Perry, "What Black Women Hear When They're Called 'Auntie,'" *Atlantic*, April 6, 2022, https://www.theatlantic.com/newsletters/archive/2022/04/auntie-word-ageism-black-women/676748/.

From My Front Porch

1 Shantell Hinton Hill, "Aunties be knowin'," *Black Girl Magic & Other Elixirs* (Baltimore: Yellow Arrow Publishing, 2023), 27.

2 This line is taken directly from Lucille Clifton, "won't you celebrate with me," in *The Book of Light* (Copper Canyon Press, 1993), 25.

Chapter 1

1 Ashé (pronounced ash-AY) is a Yoruba word signifying power and authority; typically, it is summarized to mean "May it be so."

Chapter 2

1 Assata Shakur, AZQuotes.com, Wind and Fly LTD, 2023. https://www.azquotes.com/quote/686929, accessed December 14, 2023.

Chapter 4

1 bell hooks, *The Will to Change: Men, Masculinity, and Love* (New York: Simon and Schuster, 2004), 61.

2 bell hooks, *Teaching Critical Thinking: Practical Wisdom* (New York: Routledge, 2013), 142.

Porch Talk: "Call a Thing a Thing"

1 Stacey M. Floyd-Thomas, *Black Church Studies: An Introduction* (Nashville: Abingdon Press, 2007), 142.

2 Also known as the "health and wealth" gospel, the prosperity gospel "is a fast-growing theologically conservative movement frequently associated with Pentecostalism, evangelicalism, and charismatic Christianity that emphasizes believers' abilities to

transcend poverty and/or illness through devotion and positive confession." Glossary of Terms, s.v. "Prosperity Gospel, The," Religion and Public Life at Harvard Divinity School, accessed April 29, 2024, https://rpl.hds.harvard.edu/faq/prosperity-gospel.

3 For more, see James H. Cone, *God of the Oppressed* (New York: Seabury Press, 1975).

4 Lyrics from "I'm Every Woman" as sung by Whitney Houston and Chaka Khan and written by Nickolas Ashford and Valerie Simpson. Single on Chaka Khan, *Chaka*, Warner Bros., 1978.

5 A shorter version of this poem was originally published in Shantell Hinton Hill, *Black Girl Magic & Other Elixirs* (Baltimore: Yellow Arrow Publishing, 2023), 7–10.

Chapter 6

1 If you'd like more of a deep dive into these alternative readings of Scripture having to do with homosexuality or same-gender relations, I recommend a book by Colby Martin, *UnClobber: Rethinking Our Misuse of the Bible on Homosexuality* (Louisville: Westminster John Knox, 2016), and an article by my New Testament seminary professor Amy-Jill Levine, "How to Read the Bible's 'Clobber Passages' on Homosexuality," Outreach, September 24, 2022, https://outreach.faith/2022/09/amy-jill-levine-how-to-read-the-bibles-clobber-passages-on-homosexuality/.

2 bell hooks, *Teaching Community: A Pedagogy of Hope* (New York: Routledge, 2003), 197.

Chapter 7

1 Quote attributed to Lilla Watson and other Aboriginal activist group members in Queensland, "About," Lilla: International Women's Network, last modified January 28, 2010, https://lillanetwork.wordpress.com/about/. See also "Let Us Work Together," Uniting Church in Australia, August 17, 2020, https://uniting.church/lilla-watson-let-us-work-together/.

2 Fannie Lou Hamer, "Nobody's Free Until Everybody's Free" (speech, Founding of the National Women's Political Caucus, Washington, DC, July 10, 1971).

Chapter 8

1 Tricia Hersey, *Rest Is Resistance: A Manifesto* (New York: Little, Brown Spark, 2022), 103–4.

Porch Talk: "We All We Got"
1 Chimamanda Ngozi Adichie, "The Danger of a Single Story," TedGlobal, July 2009, https://www.ted.com/talks/chimamanda_ngozi_adichie_the_danger_of_a_single_story.
2 Stacey M. Floyd-Thomas, *Black Church Studies: An Introduction* (Nashville: Abingdon Press, 2007), 143.
3 There is a time and place for calling out—for a recap, reread the Auntie-pistles and porch talk about truth-telling as spiritual discernment. Still, there is room for us to go beyond criticizing the harm and attempt to build that which we seek.
4 "Mother Teresea Reflects on Working toward Peace," Architects of Peace, last modified January 14, 2022, https://www.scu.edu/mcae/architects-of-peace/Teresa/essay.

Chapter 10
1 Corrie Pelc, "Transgender Teens 7.6 Times More Likely to Attempt Suicide," *Medical News Today*, June 14, 2022, https://www.medicalnewstoday.com/articles/transgender-teens-7-6-times-more-likely-to-attempt-suicide.
2 Pauli Murray, "The Liberation of Black Women," in *Words of Fire: An Anthology of African-American Feminist Thought*, ed. Beverly Guy-Sheftall (New York: The New Press, 1995), 197.

Chapter 11
1 "The Significant Racial Gap in Marriage Rates in the United States," *The Journal of Blacks in Higher Education*, November 21, 2022, https://jbhe.com/2022/11/the-significant-racial-gap-in-marriage-rates-in-the-united-states/.
2 Ntozake Shange, *For Colored Girls Who Have Considered Suicide/ When the Rainbow Is Enuf* (New York: Scribner, 1997), 63. First published 1975.
3 Lyvonne Briggs, *Sensual Faith: The Art of Coming Home to Your Body* (New York: Penguin Random House, 2023), 31.

Chapter 12
1 "Knuck If You Buck," on Jarques Usher, Chris Henderson, Jonathan Lewis, Venetia Lewis, and Brittany Carpentero, *Crime Mob*, Reprise Records, 2004.
2 Audre Lorde, "Eye to Eye, Black Women, Hatred, and Anger," in *Sister Outsider: Essays and Speeches* (Berkeley: Crossing Press, 2007), 171–72. First published 1984.

Porch Talk: "I Found God in Me"
1 Stacey M. Floyd-Thomas, *Black Church Studies: An Introduction* (Nashville: Abingdon Press, 2007), 143.
2 Jonathan Merritt, "One Problem with Kim Burrell's 'Hate the Sin, Love the Sinner' Argument," *USA Today*, January 4, 2017, https://www.usatoday.com/story/news/2017/01/04/kim-burrell -hate-the-sin-love-the-sinner/96158416/.
3 "Do the work your soul must have" is a phrase coined by the late womanist foremother and scholar Rev. Dr. Katie Geneva Cannon.
4 Ntozake Shange, *For Colored Girls Who Have Considered Suicide/ When the Rainbow Is Enuf* (New York: Scribner, 1997), 63. First published 1975.
5 Lines from "I'm Free," track 1 of Rev. Milton Brunson and the Thompson Community Singers, *Available to You*, Word / Epic / Sony Music Distribution, 1988.

Chapter 13
1 This and the next two quotations are from Evelyn Brooks Higgin- botham, *Righteous Discontent: The Women's Movement in the Black Baptist Church* (Cambridge: Harvard University Press, 1993), 218.
2 See, for example, the recent lawsuit at the historic Abyssinian Baptist Church where the pastoral search committee is being sued for gender discrimination: Chelsea Bailey, "Historic Black Baptist Church Sued by Woman Who Says She Wasn't Hired as Senior Pastor due to Gender Discrimination," CNN, January 9, 2024, https://www.cnn.com/2024/01/09/us/abyssinian-baptist-lawsuit -gender-discrimination-reaj/index.html.

Chapter 14
1 Excerpted from Shantell Hinton Hill, "Black girl magic," in *Black Girl Magic & Other Elixirs* (Baltimore: Yellow Arrow Publishing, 2023), 5–6.
2 Audre Lorde, "Learning from the '60s," in *Sister Outsider: Essays and Speeches (Berkeley: Crossing Press, 2007)*, 137. Lorde gave this speech at Harvard University in 1982.

Chapter 15
1 Chelsea Bailey, "Historic Black Baptist Church Sued by Woman Who Says She Wasn't Hired as Senior Pastor Due to Gender Dis- crimination," CNN, January 9, 2024, https://www.cnn.com/2024/ 01/09/us/abyssinian-baptist-lawsuit-gender-discrimination-reaj/ index.html.

2   Calvin Taylor Skinner, "Learning to Walk Alongside a Leading
    Lady: Refining My Faith as a Recovering Misogynist," *The Grio*,
    January 14, 2024, https://thegrio.com/2024/01/14/learning-to
    -walk-alongside-a-leading-lady-refining-my-faith-as-a-recovering
    -misogynist/.

Chapter 16
1   Quote taken from Ash-Lee Henderson's public Instagram page:
    https://www.instagram.com/p/C3sjAegR2y0/?img_index=1.

Porch Talk: "Make It Make Sense"
1   Stacey M. Floyd-Thomas, *Black Church Studies: An Introduction*
    (Nashville: Abingdon Press, 2007), 144.
2   I am not critiquing orthodoxy and orthopraxy. Full stop. I do not
    want to debate anyone on the importance of either. I am simply
    making a point regarding how either or both of them can hinder
    our faith development.
3   Kimberlé Crenshaw, keynote address at Women of the World 2016,
    London, March 12, 2016, https://awpc.cattcenter.iastate.edu/2018/
    09/27/keynote-at-women-of-the-world-2016-march-12-2016/.

A Benediction
1   This line is taken directly from Lucille Clifton, "won't you celebrate
    with me."

Glossary
1   Definition taken from "Dismantling Racism" website found here:
    https://www.dismantlingracism.org/racism-defined.html.
2   Alice Walker, *In Search of Our Mothers' Gardens: Womanist Prose*
    (San Diego: Harcourt Brace Jovanovich, 1983), xi–xii.
3   Summary taken from "On Womanist Theology [event description],"
    Princeton Theological Seminary, February 18, 2021, https://www
    .ptsem.edu/events/on-womanist-theology.
4   Emilie Townes, "Womanist Theology," *Union Quarterly Review* 57,
    no. 3–4 (2003): 159.
5   Stacey M. Floyd-Thomas, *Black Church Studies: An Introduction*
    (Nashville: Abingdon Press, 2007), 142–44.

The Author

Shantell Hinton Hill is a self-described Blerd (Black girl nerd) turned renaissance woman. A former engineer, she is an ordained minister in the Christian Church (Disciples of Christ). Hinton Hill works for the Winthrop Rockefeller Foundation as a narrative change and communications strategist. She has an MDiv from Vanderbilt Divinity School and is pursuing a PhD in sacred rhetoric at Clemson University. Her work and writing are situated at the intersections of social justice, storytelling, Black feminism, and womanist theology. Her body of written work includes freelance think pieces, theological essays, poetry, and short stories / memoirs. Her debut poetry collection *Black Girl Magic & Other Elixirs* was published in 2023. Connect with her on social media at @Love_Auntie.co and @ShantellHHill.